TOTAL DOPAMINE DETOX IN 7 EASY STEPS

Become the Master of Your Brain to Quit Your Phone Addiction, Porn Addiction, or Manage Your ADHD

FELIX GIROUX

Total Dopamine Detox in 7 Easy Steps

Become the Master of Your Brain to Quit Your Phone Addiction, Porn Addiction, or Manage Your ADHD

Felix Giroux

OAKRIDGE
PRESS

Contents

Introduction

Do you often feel too exhausted to lift a finger, despite having had a long period of rest? Do you often go through your days with barely any energy or motivation to get stuff done? Do you find yourself frequently fighting the urge to check your phone for notifications during work hours but end up giving in to the impulse? Not that it does you any good because you barely had any notifications at all.

The problem is that you had a feeling that you probably won't find any notifications - but you still went ahead and checked your phone. You spend the whole day waiting for a notification to "ping" your phone. Unfortunately, it doesn't feel as good as you anticipated it to be - not that it stops you from waiting for the next notification.

Now, replace waiting for notifications with any other behavior you feel you've become a little too hooked upon. It can be eating sugar or junk food, watching porn, shopping, smoking, playing video games, drinking coffee - basically, any behavior you feel is taking up too much of your time, focus, anticipation. It's now affecting your life too much that it's interfering with your productivity and success.

In hindsight, you probably know how fruitless and draining this behavior is, although it feels like it's out of your hands. Although you feel like you should give up because it's just not doing it for you anymore, you convince yourself there's just nothing you can do about it.

The truth you may be denying and struggling to accept is that you've become a borderline addict to the behavior, if not a fully-fledged addict.

Do you feel it's hopeless? And yet you want to change and take control of your life again?

Do you remember the days when you were so focused and driven that you'd always be the hardest worker in the room? Do you miss the days when you were so productive that the word "procrastination" had no meaning in your dictionary? If that is the case, I'm confident this book is exactly what you need at this point in your life.

It has been written to help you understand the root cause of all your problems, which is none other than dopamine - a neurotransmitter secreted by our brains. It may sound a little complicated at first, but that is exactly the reason I've created this book for you.

I'll help you understand the role dopamine plays in driving our desires and then take it a step further to help you realize, understand, and overcome your addictions. I'll shed light on the most common dopamine addictive activities, ranging from eating sugar to video gaming to watching pornography or even just using your smartphone.

Once you have a solid idea of how chasing the dopamine high affects your life, we'll trek through all the dopamine fasting and diets designed to reset your dopamine levels. You may be skeptical at first, but you'll soon embrace the magic of a dopamine detox once you've confirmed its efficacy.

Most of all, I'll give you a step-by-step guide to help you dopamine-detox in seven simple and straight steps. The techniques and strategies to detox your brain from dopamine overload you'll learn in this book will be here to stay. Whenever you spiral back to your old habits, you can turn back to everything you've learned in this book and take control over your life once again.

Now, are you ready to reset your life? That's the spirit!

1

Dopamine and the Role That It Plays

Dopamine is a neurotransmitter that conveys signals from your brain to other organs. For being a double-edged sword that could either drive you to pursue greatness or be the cause of your downfall, dopamine is such a cute little thing.

It's one of the driving factors pushing you to unlock achievements and pursue greater heights, which is why it's called the chemical of creativity and desire. From a different perspective, it's also one of the biggest drivers of pursuing romantic endeavors, earning its title as the chemical of love. However, it's also the biggest reason we become addicted to behaviors or even substances.

Dopamine has built a reputation for itself for being a chemical of creativity, desire, love, and addiction, but it also plays an integral role in our physical and psychological wellbeing. There are many physiological functions that dopamine regulates in human and animal bodies. It's easy to understand then how the abundance or deficit of this chemical can significantly affect an individual's well-being.

For now, let's take a closer look at this mysterious chemical to understand just how exactly it affects our lives and drives our behaviors.

What Is Dopamine?

As a neurotransmitter, dopamine acts as a chemical messenger between the neurons of the brain and the body. As a result, it helps regulate many physiological functions, which we'll get to in a bit.

Aside from its physical and mental health role, dopamine has a somewhat unique effect on the brain. Whenever your brain anticipates a reward, a surge of dopamine hits your neurons. The feeling of reward-anticipation is often triggered by doing a certain activity. Based on previous experience, the brain already knows that the end of engaging in this particular behavior feels rewarding. So even if you're still in the act of doing the behavior, the brain starts secreting dopamine.

Put simply, the brain is triggered by your behavior, whether or not it satisfies the longed-for feeling of reward. The problem arises when you reach the end of the behavior yet fail to get the "high" your brain was waiting for. When that happens, the lack of dopamine affects your brain and mood, so you end up feeling more disappointed than when you started.

To help put things into perspective, let's take an example.

There must have been a time when you were craving that sugar rush at the end of your workday. Let's say you have a fudge chocolate cake waiting for you at home, and you've been pushing through your workday for the mere reason of rewarding yourself for your hard work with none other than the majestic cake.

You wrap up your work, drive through the traffic, rush into your house, take a quick warm shower - and now you're finally ready to indulge in the fantasy you've been running all day. You open the fridge, only to find no trace of your cake. It's gone. Your wife, siblings, children, or whoever you're living with has just taken the liberty of eating the cake themselves.

Now, I know you're a completely responsible and mature grown-up who knows better than to cry for losing their sweets. That doesn't mean you wouldn't cry in this situation - I know I would. But why would a thing so trivial turn our lives upside down?

The answer will become clear once we analyze the situation.

So, what happened is that you've been fueling your dopamine all through the day. The reward was eating the chocolate cake - which you know tastes like heaven on earth. The behavior you had to get through was work - which is far from enjoyable. However, the mere thought that you'll be generously rewarded for your efforts if you just reach that endpoint was enough to motivate you to carry on and push through work.

While your dopamine levels were constantly refueling, the real hit for the brain was meant to be the reward. The exaggerated anticipation for the dopamine hit raised the dopamine baseline in your brain. So, when you failed to achieve the dopamine hit from the reward, not only did your dopamine level deteriorate, but it also fell below the normal baseline. As a result, you felt more depressed and disappointed than usual.

Now, let's say you found your chocolate cake when you returned home. You dive into the cake, and the first bite tastes exactly as you've anticipated. But then you take the second bite, and something feels wrong. Then you take the third, fourth, and fifth mouthful - but you're never able to feel the same exhilaration you had with the first bite.

Does that stop you from eating the whole cake? No way. You'll keep eating the whole cake despite not feeling all that good about it anymore.

This is what dopamine does - it keeps building up in pursuit of rewards. However, it doesn't calm down once you get your reward - if anything, it makes you yearn for more and always for some more. That's why it's also known as the "molecule of more."

This takes us to the final step to the dopamine agenda, which is the reinforcement phase. Thanks to dopamine's influence, once your brain recognizes something as pleasurable, the cycle of "motivation-reward-reinforcement" keeps repeating in an endless loop.

How Does Dopamine Make You Feel?

If we're talking about normal dopamine levels, then the right amount of dopamine will make you just perfect. You'll be in a pretty good mood, nothing extreme. However, this "good mood" helps you learn, plan, and be productive. Physiologically speaking, the right dopamine levels will help you feel alert, focused, motivated, and happy. A sudden dopamine rush will make you feel euphoric.

The Role of Dopamine

Dopamine plays an integral role in the pleasure and reward centers, but its role is far more complicated than simply being a drug wannabe. It contributes to various psychological processes that affect blood flow, sleep cycles, digestion, kidney and heart function, mood, endocrine regulation, stress response, and more.

That said, keep in mind that dopamine doesn't act alone in all of those processes. It's only able to exert its effects thanks to the help of other neurotransmitters, like adrenaline and serotonin.

So, what is exactly does the neurotransmitter dopamine do in our bodies? It's involved with regulating the following functions:

1. Movement

The basal ganglia is a part of the brain that regulates movement. However, the only way it can work at peak efficiency is by receiving a certain dose of dopamine. Without optimum dopamine levels, the movement becomes delayed and uncoordinated. On the other hand, excessive dopamine levels result in unnecessary movements, such as trembling or repetitive tics.

2. Pleasure and Reward-Seeking Behavior

We've already discussed how dopamine is the main perpetrator of pleasure-seeking activities. It drives the brain to seek pleasure and reward through different behaviors, including sex, food, gambling, and drug abuse.

3. Memory

The role of dopamine in memory is so delicate. For starters, the presence of dopamine in the prefrontal cortex, a part of the brain, is crucial in regulating and enhancing working memory. However, dopamine levels need to be accurately balanced in the prefrontal cortex. Any slight change in its level, higher or lower, affects memory considerably.

4. Attention

Dopamine also helps in attention and focus. The prefrontal cortex regulates our attention, and dopamine affects both memory and attention simultaneously. While the vision triggers the dopamine response in the brain, which diverts attention and focus on a certain subject, dopamine determines what stays in the short-term memory. It's also believed that dopamine deficiency in this area is the cause of attention deficit disorder, or ADD.

5. Cognitive Function

Dopamine is vital for an individual's cognitive function. In addition to its role in memory and attention, dopamine controls the flow of information between different brain centers. That's why any decline in dopamine levels will directly lead to neurocognitive dysfunction, which will affect memory, attention, and problem-solving skills.

6. Pain Processing

Dopamine also plays a vital role in pain processing across various parts of the brain. When dopamine levels decrease, painful symptoms are exaggerated in neurodegenerative disorders like Parkinson's disease.

7. Nausea and Vomiting

Dopamine is one of the neurotransmitters that help control nausea and vomiting. That's actually the reason some antiemetic (against nausea and vomiting) drugs are designed to trigger dopamine receptors in patients receiving chemotherapy.

8. Prolactin Secretion

Prolactin is the hormone responsible for milk production during and after pregnancy, hence why it's named after "lactation." However, it's also involved in more than 300 physiological functions, ranging from metabolic, reproductive, behavioral, fluid regulation, and immunoregulatory functions. As it happens, dopamine is one of the main regulators that inhibit prolactin secretion.

9. Social Functioning

We'll get into this in more detail in a little bit, but dopamine plays a crucial role in social functioning. Actually, people with low social phobia or even social anxiety have a reduced ability to use the dopamine they have. Meanwhile, people with high dopamine levels are usually hyper-social and hypersexual.

Dopamine Abnormalities

Dopamine abnormalities result in a wide range of problems, ranging from mild to severe. Let's take a quick look at these conditions.

- Dopamine Deficiency

Dopamine deficiency usually results in lethargy and general feelings of depression. Mildly put, you'll feel your mood is off, whether or not you can point out the reason. You may also experience the following:

- Difficulty concentrating

- Low motivation and reduced enthusiasm

- Reduced alertness

- Reduced motor skills, like poor coordination or difficulty in movement

- Sleep problems, but sleep problems also reduce dopamine levels

On a more serious note, reduced dopamine can cause serious mental and physical disorders. These include the following:

- Parkinson's disease

- Depression

- Dopamine transporter deficiency syndrome

- Dopamine Overload

Once dopamine levels increase, you'll instantly feel a strong rush of euphoria that can't be paralleled. At least, that lasts for a little while. Increased dopamine can also get you into overdrive.

However, abnormally high dopamine levels cause serious mental disorders, as it's been strongly linked to schizophrenia and psychosis. Symptoms of abnormally high dopamine include:

- Hallucinations

- Mania

- Delusions

Otherwise, high levels of dopamine can contribute to the following:

- Schizophrenia

- Obesity

- Addiction

- Addiction

In normal pathways, dopamine is secreted and re-uptaken in the brain. This process of ebb and flow is intricately maintained to balance dopamine levels at all times; as we've come to know, maintaining the delicate balance is crucial.

However, this balance is severely out of sync in addiction. Many hard drugs, like cocaine and amphetamines, mess with the dopamine pathway. Aside from hard drugs, nicotine, caffeine, alcohol, and other addictive substances also interfere with the dopamine cycle. We'll go into addiction in greater detail in the next chapter, but, for now, it's enough to understand how dopamine levels become dependent on using the substance of choice.

When this happens, the user starts losing interest in other things and becomes obsessed with chasing that high feeling. Although it may not be as physiologically severe as in the case of drug and alcohol addiction, behavioral addiction works in similar ways.

Dopamine and Evolution

You know, we're not the only creatures who have dopamine in their brains. First isolated and named in 1957, dopamine can be found in all living organisms, even the most primitive organisms. For them, it's believed that the main role dopamine plays are limited to motor control and reward enforcement learning. Those are now known to be the original primary functions of dopamine in any living organism.

However, as we've come to know, the role of dopamine is much more complex in us humans. Perhaps we've reached the top of the social hierarchy because of the higher dopamine levels we possess.

According to a report in the Proceedings of the National Academy of Sciences, humans and apes both have much higher levels of serotonin and neuropeptide Y - neurotransmitters associated with cooperative behavior and sensitivity to social cues, just like dopamine. However, the same report outlined another key difference between humans and apes: the dopamine levels. Humans had dramatically more levels of dopamine.

In other words, compared to apes, we have higher levels of dopamine that help us socialize in the complex manner we do nowadays. Scientists believe that the evolutionary pressure associated with complex social environments led to the dopamine system being used for higher and more sophisticated brain functions.

Dopamine Overload in the Digital Age

Long story short, you've been played.

We live in a digital age built on delivering instant gratification for every small action you do. Social media is an empire built on the purpose of getting you hooked for the next "like," "comment," "share," and flashy content. Every single piece of tech is designed to mess with your neurons to the extent that they fire up in excitement.

Does this sound too much like one of those conspiracy theories? Don't take it from me; take it from one of the founding presidents of Facebook, Sean Parker.

In an interview with the Guardian, Sean confessed that Facebook was created to distract us rather than connect people. He said, "The thought process was: 'How do we consume as much of your time and conscious attention as possible?'"

That's when Facebook architects decided to exploit what they deemed a "vulnerability" in human psychology. They designed their app so that everything, starting from the likes and comments you get to the pictures and posts others publish to even the colors and layout - everything on the app gives you a little dopamine hit.

You can take away Facebook and inspect any other social media app, emails, video games, or any piece of tech we had in the 20th century. They've all been built on the same idea of giving you instant dopamine hits; that's why giving them up feels so simple, yet in reality, it is difficult.

You've been programmed to chase after instant gratification even in your offline activities. You drink coffee to feel instantly awake and focused - the same goes for smoking that nicotine hit. You watch pornography to feel excited - because you can now barely feel anything without that extreme edge. You go for shopping to feel better about your image, all in anticipation of the flood of likes and comments you'll get when you post a new mirror selfie.

If only you'd take a step back and contemplate what's driving your life, you'll come to understand that it all comes down to the neurotransmitter dopamine. This tiny chemical is the reason behind your overwhelming anticipation, followed by the underwhelming satisfaction you get by engaging in the behaviors mentioned above. In short, it's the root cause for all of our behavioral addictions, as well as more serious forms of addictions.

That said, understanding addiction needs much more information - which is exactly what we'll discuss in the next chapter.

Key Takeaways

- Dopamine is the chemical of desire, creativity, love, and addiction.

- It's also the molecule of more, making you pursue pleasure and reward-seeking behavior.

- Dopamine plays an integral role in major and minor physiological and psychological functions.

- Any change in dopamine levels, to higher or lower, causes serious side effects.

- It's largely believed that dopamine is one of the biggest causes of human evolution compared to other primates.

- Thanks to how technology triggers instant gratification, almost all of us suffer from dopamine overload.

2

The Science of Addiction

Researchers have been trying to understand the nature of addiction and the natural brain chemicals that interact and influence drug use during the past decade. Nowadays, we understand the science behind addiction a lot better than ever before. We understand how broad the spectrum of substance-abuse disorders is, how our brains can be affected, and our behavior changes. Today we are more aware of the compulsive nature of drug usage and that it is now recognized as a medical disorder. Scientists are currently trying to understand possible genetic variations that may contribute to the progression or development of this disorder.

What Is Addiction?

In simple terms, addiction is a compulsive psychological or physiological need to take, to do, or use something to an extent it harms you. Addiction does not merely refer to dependence on cocaine or heroin. It also involves the complete inability to stop oneself from compulsive activities, like gambling, eating, or sex. Substance addiction is considered a chronic condition, and it may result as a side effect of some medications, often beginning with prescription opioids.

There are two categories of addiction, substance addiction, and non-substance addiction. Substance addiction involves the abuse of drugs that have psychoactive properties. In contrast, non-substance addiction includes food, gambling, the internet, cell phone, gaming, and sex. Essentially, a person suffering from the problem of addiction will continue to indulge in the activity or that substance, regardless of the harmful effects that it may have.

According to the American Society of Addiction Medicine, addiction is a treatable but chronic medical ailment involving a complex environment, life experiences, brain circuits, and genetics. In addition to this, people struggling with substance abuse disorder or an addiction problem have other comorbid psychological or physiological ailments to deal with. However, the biggest challenge for them is recognizing the need to seek help or make changes for the better in their life.

Often, people begin to indulge in drug-taking voluntarily, and gradually they become dependent on the substance, as their body reacts to repeated input of the drug, and eventually becomes unable to function without it. At this stage, a person is now a full-blown addict who cannot control their need for their drug of choice.

Differentiating Drug Misuse vs. Addiction

These two descriptive terms are often confused and thought of as describing the same thing. Drug misuse refers to misusing a substance at a high dose or misusing it in inappropriate situations leading to social or health-related issues. While this sounds quite similar to the definition of addiction, there is a fine line of difference between the two.

Not everyone who misuses a substance will have the problem of addiction. For instance, some people can consume alcohol quite heavily and may experience both the harmful and euphoric effects of alcohol. But this does not mean that they have an addiction problem unless they start undergoing a chronic episode of relapse disorder, characterized by a compulsive need to seek a drug, using the drug despite the continued harmful consequences of that substance and long-lasting neurological changes.

Addiction Symptoms and Withdrawal Effects

One of the primary indicators of an addiction problem includes poor work performance or relationship difficulties because people with an addiction problem often lash out at others around them. Signs of addiction include notice declining performance at school or difficulties staying engaged in activities. The person struggling with addiction will also not be able to stay from using a particular substance, even if it leads to personal or health-related issues. In addition, there would be a profound lack of energy in the day-to-day activities, weight loss and other changes in appearance, and lack of hygiene. The person going through this problem will become defensive, completely deny that anything is wrong, and become aggressive when confronted about this behavior.

Another classical sign of an addiction problem is having withdrawal symptoms when the person stops taking the substance or stops indulging in that behavior. These withdrawal symptoms are a group of strong symptoms that highlight the physical dependency on that substance. The withdrawal symptoms are often seen in case of sudden discontinuation of the substance of abuse (and may be fatal in some cases).

Why Do People Take Drugs?

Many reasons push people towards the slippery road to addiction. In the case of nicotine, alcohol, or other drugs, the user experiences changes in their physical and mental states that are often initially enjoyable. This then sets up an unconscious search to repeat the same euphoria. "Chasing the high" develops a dependency on these substances, and the person experiences an overpowering urge to continue using them. The activity of 'gambling' has a similar psychological effect because every time a person wins at gambling, they experience a 'high' or a 'rush' that is followed by a strong need to retry. Over time this becomes a compulsive habit that is hard to stop.

Ironically, a person's drug-taking behavior usually starts as an attempt to take control of their life, but over time it gradually robs them of that very thing. Initially, the substance of abuse seems to be an amazing solution, but it gradually becomes a pestering and debilitating problem. It also can begin as an attempt to relax, escape boredom, feel grown-up, experiment, or simply fit in. The last reason is more common among teens and young adults.

In simple words, the substance excites certain neurological pathways in the brain and generates a feeling of euphoria. However, after a while, this feeling starts fading away, and to experience the same intensity of euphoria, a higher and higher dosage is required. This obviously leads to a chronic problem and manifests as a compulsive habit that jeopardizes the person's mental and physiological health and well-being.

A person can develop strong emotional stress because of various reasons. Perhaps it is the loss of someone close, a drastic change in their financial situation, divorce, or a chronic health issue. Many people start using drugs to escape emotional turbulence or improve focus or endurance. In addition, drug users can also result from mental illness, trauma, or an attitude towards society.

Different Usage Categories

An important aspect of understanding the science behind addiction is learning about the factors or reasons that contribute to drug usage. This is because different situations may lead to a varying frequency of drug usage. Many intrinsic and extrinsic factors serve as potent contributors to the addiction issue. Another important thing to understand at this point is that these categories are not absolute distinctions because drug users tend to move from one category to another. Below are six broad categories related to the reasons for using drugs.

1. **Experimental Causes:** In this category of addiction, the person starts using the drug or substance out of pure curiosity. Over time curiosity develops into an obsessive and chronic habit that drastically undermines their well-being.

2. **Situational Factors:** A person may start using a substance to cope with situational factors o, which could be stress, feeling shy, or dealing with peer pressure.

3. **Recreational Usage:** In this category, the drug user starts taking the substance for fun and recreation, to blend in a social gathering or elevate mood.

4. **Excessing Bingeing:** According to this category, the drug user may start consuming a heavy amount of the drug for a short period of time. But over time, this becomes a recurrent habit.

5. **Therapeutic Usage:** Some drug users start taking the substance for medicinal purposes, but in the case of unmonitored dosage, it may become a problem of addiction.

6. **Dependent Usage:** This happens when a person has been using a substance in heavy doses for a long time and is already addicted. In this case, they will feel

compelled to keep taking that substance to feel normal and avoid any unpleasant withdrawal.

Common Triggers Contributing to Addiction

Before exploring the common triggers, it is important to understand the concept of 'trigger' itself.

So, what is a 'trigger'? In simple terms, it can be understood as a stimulus that would elicit a response or reaction (according to the APA dictionary, 2019). Triggers are essentially considered an important contributor to initiating the cravings for a drug or substance and will lead to increased addictive behavior. These triggers or external stimuli usually push the individual towards compulsive drug usage and can also contribute to relapse after a certain period of abstinence - either voluntary or mandatory abstinence.

While there are several psychological, emotional, and physiological reasons for people to start taking drugs, various environmental triggers or biological factors increase the likelihood of developing an addiction problem.

Below, we will review some of the reasons that may trigger or contribute to an increase in the addiction becoming a chronic problem.

1. Social Acceptability

Unfortunately, alcohol consumption is socially accepted and often lauded in our society. People drink without any hesitation at parties, and the consequences of alcohol consumption are not portrayed realistically in movies, and as a result, people are not aware of the fallout. Social gratification is a primary trigger where people unknowingly start consuming alcohol and other harmful substances. Alcohol is often front and center stage in the collective cultural conscious at parties. It has become a symbol of acceptance, and some people think they would not fit in if they did not have a glass of wine in their hands.

2. Peer Pressure

We all face peer pressure, especially during our younger years. We start doing many things to become validated by the people around us, and to do so, we start acting in the same way as they do. Peer pressure often forces people to act contrary to their personalities simply to fit in and not be seen as an outsider. This is often coupled with the need to impress others and be 'cool.'

3. Grieving a Loved One

The sudden death of someone close to you is traumatic, and it is natural to feel depressed about it. The process of recovering from such trauma is not the same for everyone. Some heal quickly and get back on track with their routines, while others struggle for several years. Such people are at great risk of being triggered to consume alcohol to dull the pain and get addicted to drugs in the hope of finding relief.

4. Going through the Loss of a Relationship

Breakups and divorces are other reasons people get addicted to drugs, especially when they do not have enough emotional support around them. Apart from just hitting the self-confidence of the person facing the breakup, it has consequences on their other relationships as well. To cope better with all the destructive events happening in their life, they find drugs as a way of getting through mourning the loss.

5. Struggling with a Psychological Illness

Psychological illnesses are not easy to handle, and when people try to deal with these issues on their own, they often end up in a mess. It is a multifaceted condition that can trigger people differently. Some will try to justify their psychological issues, while others start consuming drugs or alcohol in the hope of getting relief.

6. An Escape from Life-Stressors

We all know that life is not easy, and when a person enters into the adult phase of life, they have to learn how to deal with adult things like balancing work and home, paying off regular expenses, managing relationships, etc. Not everyone is psychologically ready to cope with these things, and some will seek peace in drug usage.

7. Environmental Influences

There is a high risk of substance abuse for people who have grown up in environments of poverty, crime, drug use, and abuse. For them, often using drugs or alcohol is a natural way of life, having never seen anything different, and the cycle is perpetuated

8. Inability to Cope with Family Demands

Most of us can deal with increasing demands from our families as we grow. However, some people don't find it easy to switch between these phases of life, especially for ambitious young mothers who become unable to pursue their careers.

9. Enhancing Performance or Focus

Some drugs have properties that can enhance your performance for a short time. People who take such drugs feel that they can always positively impact their cognition, focus, and memory. Over time, the effect of these drugs is reduced, and their usage becomes nothing more than a mere addiction.

10. Escaping Boredom

Boredom is another common trigger for drug usage. People with fewer responsibilities and more money are often using drugs to fight their boredom and monotonous lives. For them, it is a cool way of passing the time.

11. For the Fun of Getting "High"

Most drug addicts say that they started it as an experiment. Most drugs release dopamine in our bodies which is the neurotransmitter associated with feelings of pleasure. Once people experience this euphoria, they keep on taking the same drug in the hope of feeling the same thrill, and they never know when they get addicted to it.

Science of Addiction and Dopamine

Even today, a common misperception is that people who start taking drugs are either morally or psychologically weak to fall into this trap of addiction. The truth behind drug addiction is that it is quite a complex ailment and requires professional help. This is because the drugs or substances of abuse make neurological changes in the brain that make it extremely challenging for someone to stop taking drugs. Different types of drugs lead to different brain responses, and they do this because of the following:

1. These drugs usually mimic the natural neurotransmitters released in the brain. For instance, marijuana and heroin tend to imitate the response of a natural neurotransmitter, and they trick the brain receptors, activating nerve cells that usually respond to the natural neurochemicals. As the drug attaches to the receptor sites, it activates the corresponding neurons, and they send exaggerated and distorted neural messages to the CNS (central nervous system).

2. The substance of abuse, especially drugs like cocaine and methamphetamine, floods the reward circuit and leads to excessive release of a neurotransmitter, dopamine (linked with the reward system functioning in our brains). Dopamine is a potent neurotransmitter that also regulates cognition, movement, emotion, and motivation. Drugs usually generate a sudden surge of dopamine, which creates a powerful and overpowering reinforcement of the addictive behavior. In simple

terms, this strengthens the connection between pleasure and consumption of that particular substance or drug (as well as the external cues that are linked to that experience). Large sudden surges in dopamine levels teach our brains to compulsively seek that substance or drug, even at the expense of healthier goals.

3. Drugs and alcohol also disrupt our brain's chemical systems and neural circuits that control executive cognitive functions, memory, learning, stress, behavior control, decision making, and judgment. Once the physical and neurological dependency has been established, it becomes very difficult for a person to abstain from these drugs, even though they may be well aware of its harmful impact on their lives.

4.

What Happens When Someone Takes a Drug?

We all have a neurological reward system that generally controls the reinforcement of our behaviors. So, a reward system that functions properly would motivate the person to indulge in the same type of behavior repeatedly. In other words, when this reward system is activated at a normal frequency, it plays an important role in regulating our natural behaviors. However, in the case of addiction, the same reward circuit contributes to the drug-taking behavior because of the pleasure derived from taking the drug. But in doing so, it creates a strong reliance on harmful substances or drugs.

This happens because of the overstimulation of the reward circuit, leading to physical dependence with regular or consistent use of substance abuse and is a natural adaptation response of our bodies to that substance.

As the person continues to take drugs, the neural circuits in the brain change and adapt to the situation by minimizing the reward circuit cells' ability to respond to it. This, in turn, reduces the overall sensation of feeling 'high' that the drug user experienced during the first time. This phenomenon is known as 'tolerance.' To relive the same sensation after taking the substance of abuse, the users may start consuming higher doses.

The consistent neural adaptations would gradually lead to less and less pleasure from the drug or substance of abuse. Moreover, if the substance is abruptly taken away or the consumption stops, various adverse physiological symptoms can emerge, known as withdrawal symptoms.

Anticipation and Preoccupation

The effects that result from the neural changes because of the continuous use of the addictive substance often lead to obsessive anticipation or preoccupation with that substance. The drug user experiences strong cravings because the addictive substances have a stronghold on their brain and can change the brain circuitry (also known as 'conditioned reinforcement'). This, in turn, impacts the decision-making aspect and overrides their ability to make healthy choices.

Unfortunately, every time a user gives in to the triggers and takes the drug, the conditioned reinforcements are strengthened even more. Eventually, it becomes increasingly difficult to abstain from the drug. This vicious cycle creates an extremely challenging situation for the drug user.

Why Are Some People More Vulnerable than Others?

There isn't a single factor that determines the reason behind differences in addiction vulnerability because there are many factors that increase the risk of developing an addiction. This means that some people would be at more risk of developing such a problem than others. However, biology, environmental and developmental factors may play an important role in increasing the risk for some individuals.

According to research, about 40% to 60% of the risk of developing an addictive condition is because of our genetic makeup. This includes the epigenetics (effects of environmental factors on our genetic expression) and the overall family history. Also, if someone has been diagnosed with a behavioral disorder like anxiety or depression, the risk of addiction increases because it occurs as a comorbid condition with several psychological illnesses.

In a nutshell, addiction happens to be a chronic dependence on an activity, substance or drug, or alcohol and requires professional help. A person struggling with an addiction problem may have trouble abstaining from drug usage and engaging in harmful behaviors. Therefore, careful interventions and treatments must be sought.

3

Common Dopamine Addiction Activities

As we've read in the previous chapter, dopamine is the neurotransmitter that affects our experience of pleasure and the chemical released when a person is in active addiction. Our brain starts to crave that dopamine rush, and we can't stop seeking out the activity to satiate the addiction. Addicts always will experience withdrawal symptoms when quitting, even if the addiction is to a substance not considered a drug, for example, sugar, porn, video games, smartphones, and drugs and alcohol.

Not everyone who engages in these activities will become addicted. However, dopamine addictions can be incredibly destructive for those genetically or psychologically susceptible. This chapter will explore the most common dopamine addictions in more detail, including how the symptoms are displayed, the outward signs of detox and timeframes, and tips for overcoming them.

Sugar Detox

It may come as a surprise to learn that when we eat sugar, our brain releases dopamine in response to the sweet taste, just as it would if we had ingested heroin. This dopamine rush can make sugar addictive, and some people find they can't resist the urge to keep eating sweets. Sugar addiction is one of the most common dopamine addictions, and it can be incredibly damaging to our health. The detox from sugar addiction can be difficult because sugar is hidden in so many processed foods and not seen as a substance to be wary about.

The Dangers of Sugar Addiction

Sugar is linked to several health problems, including obesity, type two diabetes, heart disease, and cancer. Too much sugar can also cause mood swings, anxiety, and depression. More than two-thirds of Americans are overweight or obese, and sugar contributes to this epidemic. The major health risks associated with sugar consumption are:

- **Obesity:** Ever have that experience when you open a packet of sweets and don't stop eating them until the bag is empty? Sound familiar? The more sugar we eat, the more we want and the more likely we are to become overweight or obese. Sugar is loaded with empty calories, and it's very easy to overeat sugary foods.

- **Type 2 Diabetes:** Sugar causes our blood sugar levels to spike, leading to type two diabetes over time. Diabetes is a serious condition that can be the precursor to heart disease, stroke, blindness, and kidney failure.

- **Heart Disease:** High sugar levels in our diet can increase the risk of heart disease by raising our bad cholesterol levels and triglycerides. It can also cause inflammation, a major risk factor for heart disease.

- **Cancer:** It is believed that sugar feeds cancer cells and can promote tumor growth, although not confirmed by the authorities. However, it has been linked to several different types of cancer, including pancreatic cancer, breast cancer, and colon cancer.

- **Mood Swings:** Sugar can cause mood swings and feelings of anxiety and depression. It can also lead to a condition called hypoglycemia, which causes symptoms such as shakiness, dizziness, and sweating.

- **Other Health Problems:** Sugar can also cause headaches, tooth decay, and arthritis.

If you're addicted to sugar, you may experience cravings for sweet foods, gain weight, have mood swings, and have problems with concentration and focus. You may also feel tired and irritable and have trouble sleeping. The detox from sugar addiction can cause nausea, vomiting, and headaches. Some people also experience flu-like symptoms, such as fever, chills, and body aches.

How Sugar Addiction Manifests

Sugar addiction can manifest in many different ways. Some people become addicted to the sugar rush they get from eating sweets, while others become addicted to the comfort food provides. Some people even develop a sugar addiction to medications such as antidepressants and birth control pills. It usually starts with eating a little bit of sugar each day, but the person consumes more and more over time. Eventually, they may be eating so much sugar that it's damaging their health.

Children are particularly susceptible to sugar addiction, as their brains are still developing. The American Academy of Pediatrics recommends that children ages 2-19 should consume no more than 25 grams of sugar per day. That's about six teaspoons. For adults, the American Heart Association recommends no more than six teaspoons of sugar per day for women and nine teaspoons for men.

How to Overcome Sugar Addiction

Detoxing from sugar can be difficult, but it's not impossible. If you're struggling with sugar addiction, there are a few things you can do to help overcome it:

- **Cut Out Processed Foods**: Processed foods are loaded with sugar, so it's best to avoid them. Instead, focus on eating whole, unprocessed foods.

- **Eat a Healthy Diet:** A healthy diet is key for overcoming sugar addiction. Make sure to include plenty of fruits and vegetables, lean protein, and healthy fats in your diet.

- **Get Enough Sleep:** Getting enough sleep is essential for overcoming sugar addiction. When you're well-rested, you're less likely to crave sugar.

- **Exercise:** Exercise can help reduce cravings for sugar and other unhealthy foods. It also helps improve mood and energy levels, which can help you stay motivated to stick with your new diet and health regime.

- **Get Support:** It can be helpful to have support from family and friends when you're trying to overcome sugar addiction. Talk to them about your goals and ask for their help in supporting you. You may even find support groups in your neighborhood to join.

Duration of Sugar Detox

The detox from sugar addiction can last anywhere from a few days to a few weeks. It depends on how much sugar you're consuming and how addicted you are. The most important thing is to be patient and take it one step at a time. You'll eventually overcome your addiction if you stay focused and motivated.

Porn Detox

An unhealthy preoccupation with internet pornography is far more concerning than you might imagine. It's a real addiction, and it's just like any other addiction. You can't control how much you use it, when you use it, or how long you use it. It consumes your mind so much that you feel compelled to think about it and want to do nothing else. It harms your relationships with others. It damages your social life and ability to interact with people in the real world. But worst of all, it damages your ability to be intimate with another person and have a loving relationship.

The Dangers of Porn

It affects your physical health in a lot of negative ways. It leaves you feeling terrible when you stop using it and makes you feel better when you are using it (though not as good as you think; your brain just tricks you into thinking so). It damages your work performance. It causes a lot of procrastination and distraction from doing what needs to be done in life. It takes up time that could be spent on more important things.

Being dependent on porn for your pleasure damages your spirituality by desensitizing you to beauty, love, and compassion. It makes you view people as objects for your gratification, rather than viewing them as fellow human beings. While there are countless negative implications of porn on your mental health, it can also lead to erectile dysfunction. Despite knowing that it's hurting their relationships, health, and productivity, many people can't seem to break the habit.

Symptoms

Compulsive sexual activities characterize sexual addiction despite all the negative consequences. Although there is no official diagnosis for sexual addiction, clinicians and researchers have attempted to define the disorder using criteria based on chemical dependency literature. Symptoms include preoccupation with sexual fantasies, urges, and behaviors, engaging in these activities in response to dysphoric mood states (anxiety, sadness, boredom), engaging in these behaviors despite potential harm to oneself or others, and an inability of the individual to control these impulses.

Detoxing from Porn Addiction

Firstly, get a good understanding of what sexual addiction is. Read relevant books and articles. If you have never heard of the concept before, knowing that there is information out there will probably be very helpful and hopeful. The more you understand porn addiction, the better. The more you know about something, the less it has power over you. There's no magic bullet here. It will take time, energy, and commitment to make it happen. Some guidelines can help you along the way:

- Know your triggers. If you know what triggers your addictive behavior, it'll be easier to avoid them or deal with their effects.

- Be aware of your feelings and emotions. This can help you learn more about yourself and what's causing you to seek out addiction as a coping mechanism.

- Seek support from others who can relate to porn addiction. Support groups are especially helpful for this purpose.

- Maintain a healthy lifestyle by eating a balanced diet, getting enough sleep, staying active, and managing stress levels.

- Learn new coping skills and strategies such as meditation, yoga, and mindfulness training.

Video Games Detox

Video game addiction is a type of behavioral addiction that manifests in an obsessive-compulsive need to play video games. People addicted to video games spend hours playing them every day, to the detriment of their relationships, work, and school. Video game addiction is a real phenomenon, and it's becoming more and more prevalent. According to the National Center for Biotechnology Information, 9% of men and 6% of women in the United States are addicted to video games.

Widespread video gaming addiction is a relatively new phenomenon, and there is still much to learn about it. Teenagers are particularly susceptible to it. According to a study by the University of Texas at Austin, 88% of American teenagers play video games, and 60% of those who play video games play for three or more hours per day.

The Implications of Video Games Addiction

Video games addiction can have several negative consequences. People who are addicted to video games may neglect their work, school, and relationships. They may also suffer from health problems due to playing video games for long periods, such as carpal tunnel syndrome, poor vision, and obesity. Apart from the negative consequences for the individual, video gaming addiction can also harm society as a whole.

Excessive video gaming can lead to social isolation and violence. While there is still much to learn about this addiction, it is clear it can have serious consequences. For those who are addicted to video games, there is hope. There are treatment options available that can help people overcome their addiction.

People who are addicted to video games may exhibit the following symptoms:

- **Obsessive Thoughts:** Addicts may constantly think about playing video games. They may feel like they can't concentrate on anything else until they've played.

- **Tolerance:** Those addicted to video games may need to play for longer periods to achieve the same level of satisfaction.

- **Withdrawal:** Addicts will experience withdrawal symptoms when they can't play, just as any other addict would. These symptoms may include anxiety, irritability, bad temper, and depression.

- **Loss of Interest in Other Activities:** Those addicted to video games may lose interest in other activities, such as spending time with friends and family or going to the gym.

- **Continual Use:** People addicted to video games may play for hours at a time, sometimes even skipping meals and going without sleep.

How Video Game Addiction Manifests

How video game addiction manifests varies from person to person. Some people may be more likely to isolate themselves from friends and family and play video games for hours on end, while others may be more likely to become aggressive and can become violent. There are many different ways in which video game addiction can be exhibited.

For some individuals, video gaming addiction can have serious consequences. For example, they can lose their job or fall completely behind in school work because of the amount of time they spend playing games. They may also experience health problems as a result of playing video games for long periods, including back pain, carpal tunnel syndrome, and poor vision.

Some withdrawal symptoms, such as anxiety and depression, are common to many addictions. However, other withdrawal symptoms, such as increased aggression, may be specific to video game addiction. It's critical to understand how video game addiction appears in each individual when attempting to overcome it. This will help the individual to address the problem and seek treatment.

Detoxing from Video Game Addiction

There is no one-size-fits-all approach to detoxing from video game addiction. Some people may need to attend an inpatient treatment center, while others may be able to overcome their addiction with the help of outpatient therapy. The detox process will vary depending on the person and their addiction. However, a few general things can help during the detox from video game addiction.

- **Seek Professional Help:** During the detox procedure, it's critical to get expert aid. Ensure that you have the support you need to overcome your addiction.

- **Cut off All Access to Video Games:** This may seem like an obvious step, but it's important to do. If you have any video games, consoles, or other devices that allow you to play video games, get rid of them.

- **Replace Video Games with Other Activities:** Fill your time with activities that have nothing to do with technology. This may include going for walks, reading, watching movies, or spending time with friends and family.

- **Create a New Routine:** When you're detoxing from video game addiction, take your time creating a new routine. The goal is to prevent yourself from turning to video games as a crutch.

- **Be Patient:** Detoxing from any addiction can be difficult. Be patient with yourself and know that you can overcome this addiction.

Timeframe for Detoxing from Video Game Addiction

The time it takes to detox from video game addiction varies from person to person. Some people may need only a few weeks to get over their addiction, while others may need several months. Success depends on many factors, like the severity of the addiction and the support available from family and friends. The detox process will require time and effort. Don't be discouraged if you don't overcome your addiction overnight. With the right help and support, you can overcome video game addiction.

Smartphone Addiction

Smartphones are an important part of our lives, but they can be addictive like anything else. Most people would agree that we rely on our smartphones too much and use them for things that we really shouldn't. Constantly checking our phones has become the norm, even when we are in company and some societies no longer consider it ill-mannered.

When we're not using our phones, we're thinking about them. We can't stop ourselves from constantly checking for new notifications, messages, and emails. And when we're not using our phones, we feel anxious and lost without them. This is what addiction looks like.

Smartphone addiction isn't recognized as an official disorder, but it's a real problem. And it's only going to get worse as we become more and more reliant on our phones.

The Reality of Smartphone Addiction

Most people don't think of themselves as being addicted to their smartphones. But the reality is that many of us are. The dangers that smartphone addiction pose are real and should not be ignored. Some of the dangers of smartphone addiction include:

- **Decreased Productivity:** When we're constantly checking our phones, we're not getting things done. We're distracted, and our productivity suffers.

- **Increased Stress:** Checking our phones for new notifications causes us stress. We constantly feel the need to be connected, which causes a lot of anxiety.

- **Damaged Relationships:** We're spending less time with our friends and family because we're glued to our phones. This can damage relationships.

- **Negative Effects on Mental Health:** Smartphones can harm our mental health. We may experience anxiety, depression, and even psychosis.

- **Physical Health Problems:** Smartphones can also cause physical health problems. We're more likely to get sick because we're not getting enough sleep or exercise and are constantly stressed.

- **Dangers While Driving:** Smartphones can be dangerous while driving. We're more likely to get into accidents because we're not paying attention to the road.

How Smartphone Addiction Manifests

Smartphone addiction displays in different ways for different people. For some, the addiction may be seen in the amount of time they spend on their phone. They may be on their phone for hours at a time and not realize how much time has passed. For others, the addiction may be more subtle. They may only check their phone a few times an hour, but they need to do it is overwhelming.

There are also different ways that people use their smartphones. Some people use their phones to stay connected with friends and family, while others use them to pass the time. Some people use their phones to escape from reality. Smartphones provide a sense of comfort and escape for these people.

How to Overcome Smartphone Addiction

Once you realize that you're addicted to your smartphone, it's time to take action. Here are a few steps that you can take to overcome your addiction:

- **Make Changes to Your Phone Habits**: The first step is to change your phone habits. You need to be more mindful of how you're using your phone. Try to limit the amount of time you spend on your phone and be more intentional about how you're using it.

- **Disconnect from Your Phone:** Another way to overcome your addiction is to disconnect from your phone. This means turning off your notifications, putting your phone away, and not using it when you're with friends and family.

- **Find Other Ways to Connect:** Instead of relying on your phone to stay connected with friends and family, find other ways to connect. Spend time talking to them in person or try a messaging app that allows you to have group chats.

- **Find Other Ways to Pass the Time**: If you're using your phone to pass the time, find other ways to do that. Read a book, watch a movie, or go for a walk.

- **Get Enough Sleep:** One of the best ways to overcome smartphone addiction is to get enough sleep. When you're tired, you're more likely to reach for your phone.

- **Seek Professional Help:** If you can't overcome your addiction on your own, seek professional help. Many therapists specialize in smartphone addiction.

Drug and Alcohol Detox

Detoxing from drugs or alcohol can be a difficult process. It can be dangerous, and it's essential to seek professional help. Unlike other addictions, detoxing from drugs or alcohol can be life-threatening. When you detox from drugs or alcohol, your body goes through withdrawal. This means that you'll experience a variety of symptoms, some of which can be dangerous.

The detox process usually lasts for a few weeks, or others can take as long as six months. However, it may take longer for some people. The length of the detox process depends on what you're addicted to and how long you've been using it. The detox process can be difficult to manage on your own and is not recommended. A professional can monitor your progress and make sure that you're safe. They can also provide you with support and guidance.

How Drug and Alcohol Addictions Manifest

Drug and alcohol addiction is seen in different ways. Some people may become addicted to drugs or alcohol after using them for a short period. Others may use drugs or alcohol as a way to cope with stress or anxiety. When you're addicted to drugs or alcohol, you'll continue to use them, even if it's causing problems in your life.

According to the National Institute on Drug Abuse, addiction is a "chronic, relapsing brain disease," meaning addiction is a lifelong disease that you'll need to manage. There's no cure for addiction, but there are treatments available that can help you manage your disease.

Symptoms of Drug and Alcohol Addiction

The symptoms of drug and alcohol addiction can vary from person to person. However, there are some common symptoms that you may experience:

- **Tolerance:** This means that you need to use more of the drug or alcohol to get the same effect.

- **Withdrawal:** When you stop using the drug or alcohol, you'll experience withdrawal symptoms.

- **Craving:** You'll continue to crave the drug or alcohol, even if you're aware of the negative consequences it's causing in your life.

- **Loss of Control:** You'll lose control over your use of drugs or alcohol, and you'll be unable to stop using them, even if you want to.

- **Social Withdrawal:** You'll withdraw from your friends and family, and you'll spend more time using drugs or alcohol.

- **Financial Problems:** You'll have financial problems due to your addiction.

- **Legal Problems:** You may get into legal troubles due to your addiction.

- **Emotional Problems:** You'll experience a variety of emotional problems, such as depression, anxiety, and paranoia.

- **Physical Problems:** You'll experience a variety of physical problems due to your addiction.

How to Detox from Drugs or Alcohol

There are many different types of drug and alcohol addictions. Some people may be addicted to prescription drugs, while others may be addicted to street drugs. Some people may be addicted to alcohol, while others may be addicted to marijuana. Drug and alcohol addiction can be a difficult disease to overcome. However, with the help of a professional and a 12 step program, you can manage your addiction and live a healthy life. Here's a look at how to detox from drugs or alcohol:

- **Talk to Your Doctor:** Talk to your doctor about the best way to detox from your drug or alcohol addiction. They may recommend a specific detox program, or they may prescribe you medication to help you detox.

- **Enter a Detox Program:** There are many different types of detox programs available. Choose the program that's best for you and your needs.

- **Detox in a Safe Environment:** Make sure the detox program you choose is staffed by medical professionals who can monitor your progress and ensure your safety.

- **Detox Slowly:** Don't try to detox from drugs or alcohol quickly. Detoxing too quickly can be dangerous and may cause you to relapse. Detox slowly over some time to ensure your safety.

- **Seek Professional Help:** Seek professional help during and after detox. A professional can provide you with the support and guidance you need to manage your addiction.

Depending on the type of drug or alcohol addiction you have, detox can take anywhere from a few days to a few weeks. Follow your doctor's instructions and seek professional help to ensure a safe and successful detox.

Gambling Detox

Gambling addiction, or pathological gambling, is a type of addiction that involves gambling compulsively. You may feel an urge to gamble more and more money, even if you're aware of the negative consequences it's causing in your life. There are cases where people have lost their homes, jobs, and families as a result of gambling addiction.

Based on the National Council on Problem Gambling, there are an estimated two million problem gamblers in the United States. And while gambling addiction is less talked about than other addictions like drugs or alcohol, it can be just as damaging. The consequences of gambling addiction can be disastrous, causing financial, legal, and emotional problems.

How Gambling Addiction Manifests

Gambling addiction can manifest in many different ways. Some people gamble compulsively, while others only gamble occasionally. Some people gamble for fun, while others gamble to escape their problems. Gambling addiction can be a dangerous disease that can cause a lot of damage in your life. Here are some of the most common symptoms:

- **Gambling More than You Can Afford:** You'll gamble more money than you can afford, even if it means going into debt or taking out loans.

- **Losing Control:** You'll lose control over your gambling, and you'll be unable to stop, even if you want to.

- **Gambling despite Negative Consequences:** You'll gamble even if you know the negative consequences it's causing in your life.

- **Gambling to Escape Problems:** You'll gamble as a way to escape your problems or to relieve boredom or stress.

- **Telling Lies to Cover up Gambling:** You'll lie to friends and family to cover up your gambling.

- **Feeling Anxious or Depressed:** You'll feel anxious or depressed due to your gambling addiction.

How to Detox from a Gambling Addiction

To detox from gambling addiction, you'll need to seek professional help. There are many different programs and treatments available for pathological gambling. Here's a look at some of the most common treatments:

- **Cognitive-Behavioral Therapy**: This type of therapy helps you change your thoughts and behaviors associated with gambling. Part of the program is meeting with a therapist regularly to talk about your addiction and how to overcome it. They may also give you homework assignments to help you change your thoughts and behaviors.

- **Group Therapy:** Group therapy is a type of therapy where you meet with a group of people who are struggling with the same addiction as you, allowing you to share your experiences and learn from others, which is often very helpful.

- **Medication:** There are medications available that can help you overcome gambling addiction. These medications work by reducing the cravings and urges to gamble. The most common medication used for gambling addiction is naltrexone.

- **Rehabilitation:** Rehabilitation is a type of treatment where you live at a rehab center for some time. This type of treatment can be helpful for people who have a severe gambling addiction. The rehab center will provide you with counseling and therapy, as well as support to overcome your addiction.

- **Online Self-Help Forums**: There are self-help groups available for people struggling with gambling addiction. These groups allow you to share your experiences with other people who are struggling with the same addiction. They can help get support and advice without leaving home.

Pathological gambling is a type of impulse-control disorder that affects millions of people worldwide. It's still a gambling addiction, and it can be just as damaging as any other addiction. The consequences of gambling addiction can be far-reaching and can cause a lot of damage to your life. Gambling addiction can be a difficult addiction to overcome, but you can overcome it with the help of a professional. Seek out a program that fits your needs and stick with it. For more information, please contact your local addiction center.

Key Takeaways

Many different addictions can involve dopamine, but this chapter discussed some of the most common dopamine addictions. Here is a list of the most important things to remember from this chapter:

- Dopamine is a neurotransmitter that is associated with pleasure and reward.

- Addictions can involve dopamine because they provide a rush of pleasure that is addictive.

- The most common dopamine addictions are sugar, porn, video games, smartphones, drugs, alcohol, and gambling.

- To detox from sugar addiction, replace sugar with healthy foods and monitor your sugar intake.

- To detox from porn addiction, abstain from watching porn and seek professional help.

- To detox from video game addiction, limit the amount of time you spend playing video games and replace video games with other activities.

- To detox from smartphone addiction, limit the amount of time you spend on your smartphone and replace smartphone use with other activities.

- To detox from drug and alcohol addiction, seek professional help and go through a detox program.

- To detox from gambling addiction, seek professional help and go through a detox program.

- The most common treatments for dopamine addictions are cognitive-behavioral therapy, group therapy, medication, rehabilitation, and online self-help forums.

If you are struggling with a dopamine addiction, consult a verified professional. There are many different programs and treatments available for dopamine addictions. Choose the program that is best for you and stick with it. It will be a difficult journey, but it's worth it in the end.

4

Dopamine Fasting and Diets

In the last few years, there's been a lot of talk about dopamine fasting and what it means to abstain from pleasurable activities. If you're not familiar with it, dopamine fasting is the practice of depriving yourself of pleasurable experiences like eating, drinking, and social media. The idea is that the temporary deprivation will help reset your brain to control your impulses more easily.

The fad has been covered by several high-profile outlets like The New York Times, but some experts have sharply criticized the concept as lacking a scientific basis.

But what if you're still interested in giving it a try? What does dopamine fasting mean for your diet?

If you're struggling with an addiction to dopamine or simply want to reset your body's internal clock (so to speak), there are several methods you can try. These include dopamine fasting and dopamine diets. This chapter will explain what dopamine fasting is before going into the benefits of this practice. This chapter will also discuss adjusting your nutrition for dopamine fasting and whether it's worth trying this approach. Finally, we'll take a look at some of the most popular dopamine diets and how they differ from one another.

What Is Dopamine Fasting?

Addiction to certain foods can be just as powerful as addiction to drugs or alcohol. Sugar, salt, and processed foods are all common culprits. While it's not always easy to break the addiction, dopamine fasting may provide a way to do just that.

Dopamine fasting is a type of fasting designed to help you break your addiction to it. It involves limiting the number of things that stimulate dopamine release. This practice can also involve periods without technology, social media, sex, or food.

Dopamine fasting can help decrease the brain's dependence on external sources to get its "fix." It can increase your ability to generate dopamine through internal sources, as well as boost your ability to regulate dopamine levels yourself. It has also been known to increase motivation, creativity, empathy, and general outlook on life.

For most people, the idea of a "dopamine fast" sounds like something that could only be achieved by a monk who has spent a lifetime trying to quiet their mind. But in fact, our brains are constantly releasing dopamine, the chemical that gives us feelings of pleasure and motivation.

You might think that's not a bad thing, but according to some researchers, we're living in an age where we're constantly bombarded with pleasurable stimuli. This causes many people to crave these things more often or in greater quantity than they should. This inevitably can lead to problems such as obesity and addiction.

You can't stop your brain from releasing dopamine, but the concept of fasting is about restricting the things that cause it to be released so you can regain your sensitivity to those things. There's nothing wrong with enjoying these things in moderation, but when they become a crutch, they can be difficult to break free from. That's where dopamine fasting comes in.

How to Adjust Nutrition for Dopamine Fasting

There is no one perfect diet for dopamine fasting. However, you can do a few general things to adjust your nutrition and make the experience more beneficial.

1. **Reduce Your Intake of Sugar, Processed Foods, and Caffeine**

    Processed foods, sugar, and caffeine are all known to stimulate dopamine release. Try to reduce your intake of these things while fasting. Always check the ingredients list on food labels and avoid anything with sugar, high fructose corn syrup, or artificial sweeteners. The same goes for caffeine. Try to avoid coffee, tea, and energy drinks while dopamine fasting. It helps to have a plan for what you will eat instead of these things.

2. Eat More Whole Foods

Whole foods are less processed and contain more nutrients than processed foods. They also tend to have a lower glycemic index, meaning they won't cause blood sugar spikes. Try to make at least 50% of your diet whole foods by including things like fruits, vegetables, whole grains, and lean proteins. You can also try to eat mindfully by paying attention to how you're feeling after eating different foods. If you feel good after eating a certain food, it's likely a good choice for dopamine fasting.

3. Drink Plenty of Fluids

Fluids are important because they help to flush toxins from the body. Try to drink plenty of water, herbal teas, and detox drinks. Avoid caffeine and alcohol, as they are dehydrating. It's also essential to get plenty of electrolytes, especially if you're doing a lot of exercise. Coconut water and sports drinks are good sources of electrolytes.

4. Avoid Foods That Cause Intolerance or Allergy

Certain foods can cause inflammation in the body and lead to problems such as gas, bloating, and diarrhea. If you find that you have a food intolerance or allergy, avoid those foods while dopamine fasting. Fast-food restaurants are a common source of these foods.

Burgers, fries, and pizza are all high in fat, sugar, and salt. They're also loaded with chemicals that can trigger inflammation.

5. Supplement with Omega-3s

Omega-3 fatty acids are important for overall health and can help to reduce inflammation. They're especially beneficial for people who are on dopamine fast. Try to supplement with a quality omega-3 supplement. Foods high in omega-3s include salmon, walnuts, chia seeds, and flaxseeds. Other good sources of omega-3s include fish oil supplements and algae supplements.

6. Take a Probiotic

A probiotic is a good way to support gut health while dopamine fasting. The gut is home to trillions of bacteria, some of which are beneficial and some are not. Probiotics help to maintain a healthy balance of bacteria in the gut. They can also help to reduce inflammation and improve digestion. Look for a probiotic that contains multiple strains of bacteria.

7. Avoid Foods that Are High in Lectins

Lectins are proteins found in many plant foods. They can cause inflammation and digestive problems. Foods that are high in lectins should be avoided while dopamine fasting. These foods include grains, legumes, and nightshade vegetables. Instead, focus on eating nutrient-rich fruits and vegetables.

8. Eat More Fermented Foods

Fermented foods are high in probiotics and can help to support gut health. They're also a good source of the enzymes essential for digestion. Try to include fermented foods in your diet while dopamine fasting. Some good options include sauerkraut, kimchi, yogurt, and kefir.

9. Increase Your Intake of Healthy Fats

Healthy fats are essential for overall health. They help support the immune system, reduce inflammation, and improve brain function. While fasting, increase your intake of healthy fats by eating things like nuts, seeds, avocado, and olive oil. You can also drink smoothies made with healthy fats.

10.   Avoid Eating Late at Night

Eating late at night can interfere with your sleep and sabotage your dopamine fasting efforts. Try to avoid eating after 8 pm. If you need a snack late at night, choose something light like a small bowl of yogurt or a piece of fruit. Thoroughly chew all food to help with digestion. Make it a habit to eat slowly and mindfully, even when you're not fasting.

11. Exercise Regularly

Exercise is a great way to boost overall health and well-being. It's also beneficial for people who are on dopamine fast. Regular exercise can help to reduce inflammation, improve mood, and boost energy levels. Include at least 30 minutes of exercise most days of the week. It also helps to break up the monotony of dieting. Try different types of exercise to keep things interesting.

12. Practice Mindfulness

Mindfulness is a form of meditation that can help to improve mental well-being. It's also beneficial for people who are fasting. Mindfulness helps to reduce stress, anxiety, and depression. It can also improve focus and concentration. To practice mindfulness, find a quiet place to sit or recline. Close your eyes and focus on your breath. Notice the thoughts and feelings that come up, but don't judge them. Practice for 10-15 minutes per day.

The Benefits of Dopamine Fasting

While dopamine fasting may seem like a new trend, there is some evidence to suggest that it can be beneficial for overall health. Here are some of the benefits that have been reported:

1. Improved Mental Clarity and Focus

One of the main benefits is improved mental clarity and focus. Dopamine fasting eliminates processed foods and unhealthy sugar from the diet. When the body is not bombarded with processed foods, it has a chance to reset and function more effectively. With only healthy, nutrient-rich foods being consumed, the mind focuses better and thinks more clearly.

2. Reduced Inflammation

Chronic inflammation is linked to several health problems, including heart disease, cancer, and arthritis. Reducing inflammation is essential for overall health. Dopamine fasting can help to reduce inflammation due to the elimination of processed foods and the addition of healthy fats. The anti-inflammatory effects will be even greater if you take additional supplements while dopamine fasting, such as fish oil or turmeric.

3. Weight Loss

This type of fast is also an effective way to lose weight. When you eliminate processed foods and focus on eating nutrient-rich foods, weight loss is inevitable. The best part is that dopamine fasting is that it is a sustainable way to lose weight and keep it off. Eating this way is not a fad diet but a healthy, long-term way of eating.

4. Improved Mood

Processed foods are known to have a negative effect on your mood. When you eliminate these foods and focus on eating healthy, nutrient-rich foods, your mood will improve. The body will no longer be in a state of toxicity and will be able to function at its best. You'll find that you have more energy and are less likely to experience mood swings.

5. Improved Digestion

Eating processed foods can wreak havoc on the digestive system. Your digestion will improve when you stop consuming these foods and focus on eating healthy, fiber-rich foods. By incorporating regular exercise into your dopamine fasting routine, you'll be on your way to optimal digestion. Sustained weight loss is also linked to better digestion.

6. Increased Energy Levels

Processed foods are high in sugar and caffeine, leading to a crash in energy levels. When you eliminate these foods and focus on eating healthy, nutrient-rich foods, your energy levels will increase. You'll find that you have more sustained energy throughout the day and are less likely to experience a mid-afternoon slump. Many people also report that they have more energy when they exercise while dopamine fasting.

7. Better Skin

Your skin is your body's largest organ, and it's vital to take care of it. Processed foods can harm skin health-inducing wrinkles, blemishes, and dryness. You will find that incorporating healthy, nutrient-rich foods into your diet will result in your skin being less oily, acne is reduced, and wrinkles are less noticeable.

8. Reduced Risk of Disease

Eating processed foods increases the risk of developing chronic diseases such as heart disease, cancer, and diabetes. Excess inflammation and the consumption of unhealthy sugar are to blame. Dopamine fasting can help to reduce the risk of developing these diseases due to its anti-inflammatory effects and the focus on eating healthy, nutrient-rich foods.

9. Better Sleep

Processed foods can interfere with sleep quality and quantity. Irregular sleep patterns are linked to several health problems, including weight gain and an increased risk of disease. Healthy foods like those found in a dopamine fasting diet help to promote good sleep habits. You'll find that you fall asleep more easily and sleep through the night without waking up.

10.   Increased Lifespan

Studies have shown that a healthy diet can increase lifespan. Setting yourself up for a longer, healthier life requires eating nutrient-rich foods. Going on a dopamine fast is one way to do this. The benefits are vast and include improved mental clarity, reduced inflammation, weight loss, improved mood, and better digestion. It's worth giving it a try not only to get over addictive behavior but also to simply start living a healthier and better life.

Diets for Dopamine Fasting

Many different diets can be followed while dopamine fasting. Here are a few of the most popular ones:

1. Paleo Diet

The Paleo diet is based on the idea that humans are best suited to eat the same foods as our Paleolithic ancestors, meaning that processed foods, dairy, grains, and legumes are all off-limits. The Paleo diet focuses on eating a nutrient-rich diet with foods like fruits, vegetables, meat, poultry, seafood, and eggs. A few modifications can be made to the Paleo diet while dopamine fasting, such as avoiding starchy vegetables and consuming more healthy fats.

2. Mediterranean Diet

The Mediterranean diet is based on the traditional diet of countries bordering the Mediterranean Sea. It is high in fruits, vegetables, whole grains, legumes, fish, and healthy fats and low in meat and processed foods. The Mediterranean diet is a good option for dopamine fasting as it is nutrient-rich and allows for some flexibility in what you can eat. If you follow a vegetarian or vegan version of the Mediterranean diet, you can still reap its benefits while dopamine fasting.

3. Vegetarian Diet

A vegetarian diet eliminates all animal products, including meat, poultry, seafood, and eggs. There are many different types of vegetarian diets, but most focus on eating a variety of fruits, vegetables, whole grains, and legumes. A vegetarian diet can be followed while dopamine fasting with a few modifications, such as avoiding starchy vegetables and consuming more healthy fats. You may find you have more energy and better digestion when following a vegetarian diet while dopamine fasting.

4. Vegan Diet

Vegans consume only plant-based foods, eliminating all animal products, including meat, poultry, seafood, eggs, and dairy. Vegans may find it harder to stick to a healthy diet while dopamine fasting as fewer options are available. However, following a healthy vegan diet while dopamine fasting with some creativity is possible with some creativity. Try focusing on nutrient-rich foods like bananas, sweet potatoes, quinoa, and chia seeds.

5. Ketogenic Diet

The ketogenic diet is a high-fat, low-carbohydrate diet that helps to induce ketosis, a state in which the body uses fat for energy instead of carbohydrates. A ketogenic diet is a good option for dopamine fasting as it is very restrictive and limits the number of unhealthy foods that can be eaten. However, it can be difficult to follow and may not suit everyone.

6. Low-Carbohydrate Diet

A low-carbohydrate diet is a diet that restricts the number of carbohydrates eaten. Low-carbohydrate diets are popular for weight loss and are effective for dopamine fasting. There are many different types of low-carbohydrate diets, but most focus on eating a variety of healthy meats, vegetables, and fruits.

7. Macronutrient Diet

A macronutrient diet focuses on the ratio of macronutrients eaten, such as carbohydrates, proteins, and fats. A macronutrient diet can be followed while fasting, but make sure that the majority of your calories come from healthy sources like fruits, vegetables, and whole grains. Foods like candy and fast food should be avoided on this diet.

8. Intermittent Fasting

Intermittent fasting is an eating pattern where you eat during a specific time window and then fast for the rest of the day. Intermittent fasting can be followed while on dopamine fast, but make sure you get the right nutrients during your feeding window. Try to focus on nutrient-rich foods like fruits, vegetables, and whole grains during your feeding window.

9. Juice Fast

A juice fast is a type of fast where all the food eaten is juice. A juice fast can be followed while fasting if you include plenty of nutrient-rich fruits and vegetables in your juice recipes. It's a good way to detoxify your body and get a variety of nutrients. This diet is not recommended for people with a history of eating disorders.

10.   Bone Broth Fast

A bone broth fast is a type of fast where all the food eaten is bone broth. Bone broth is a good source of protein and other nutrients, making it a healthy choice for a fast. If you include plenty of vegetables in your recipes, it ensures you get the nutrients you need while dopamine fasting. Keto-adapted athletes often use bone broth fasts to increase ketone levels and improve athletic performance.

Is Dopamine Fasting a Fad?

Dopamine fasting is a relatively new trend, and there is still some uncertainty about whether it works. However, there is growing evidence that it can be an effective way to lose weight and improve health. Many different diets can be followed, making it a versatile and flexible approach to healthy eating. It can't be considered a fad because it has been around for a while, continues to grow in popularity, and it works. Once more research is conducted on dopamine fasting, this approach to healthy eating will likely become more mainstream.

Key Takeaways

Here's a recap of the things discussed in this chapter:

- Dopamine fasting is a diet and fasting approach that focuses on limiting the amount of dopamine-inducing foods eaten.

- There are many different types of dopamine-fasting diets, but most focus on eating a variety of healthy foods like fruits, vegetables, and whole grains.

- To adjust nutrition for dopamine fasting, focus on eating nutrient-rich foods like fruits, vegetables, and whole grains. Avoid unhealthy foods like candy and fast food.

- The benefits of dopamine fasting include weight loss, improved health, increased energy, better mental clarity, and better sleep.

- There is still some uncertainty about whether dopamine fasting works, but there is growing evidence that it can be an effective way to lose weight and improve health.

- Many different diets can be followed while dopamine fasting, making it a versatile and flexible approach to healthy eating.

- Dopamine fasting is not a fad but rather a trend growing in popularity. More research is needed to determine the full effects of dopamine fasting.

- Dopamine fasting can be followed while following other types of diets, as long as most of your calories come from healthy foods.

- Intermittent fasting, juice fasting, and bone broth fasting are all types of dopamine fasting that can be followed.

With so many different dopamine-fasting diets to choose from, it can be difficult to know which one is right for you. Find a diet that fits your lifestyle and that you can stick to. If you're not sure where to start, try one of the dopamine-fasting diets listed above. And always consult with a doctor before starting any new diet.

5

The Benefits of a Dopamine Detox

Now that you have learned about the different dopamine fasting techniques and diets, you may be wondering if there are any genuine advantages to a dopamine detox. After all, detaching yourself from impulsive behaviors and denying yourself instant gratification is hard work, so surely it must come with some benefits? Fortunately, it does. In fact, the benefits go far beyond just giving us the ability to stop engaging in mindless behavior - such as binge-watching our favorite TV shows and scrolling on social media - which is what most people aim to achieve by activating dopamine detox.

That said, you can't expect to find the solution to all your issues in dopamine detox. Nor can you avoid every problem, event, situation, or person that causes them either. Doing this would hamper the normal release of dopamine, taking things too far and presenting an entirely new set of issues. So, it's a good idea to focus on achieving the benefits in smaller increments. Keep in mind that a "quick fix' approach always leads to short-term results. If we want to avoid every activity that distracts us from our goals, we must put in the long-term work to actively avoid them. And this is what we will be discussing in this chapter.

Freedom from Distractions

We live in a society where distractions can be found everywhere in our daily lives, and we seemingly gain great joy from them. It's only by distancing ourselves from this culture that we begin to realize just how false this happiness is. As our brains detox from dopamine, we become aware that this hormone only amplifies all those activities we seem to enjoy. It isn't called the molecule of more for no reason. The more we engaged in activities we felt gratifying, the more dopamine encouraged us to continue seeking a repetition.

Unfortunately, these types of distractions are detrimental to personal and professional growth. And when our brain no longer produces such a high amount of dopamine, we can see that dopamine isn't giving us happiness. It only provides us with a motivation that follows pleasure - but only if the reason was instant gratification. Now liberated from these distractions, we can pursue other values that are far more beneficial for our mind and life in general.

The culture of distraction is one many people around us are involved in, making it even harder to break away from it. But as you will soon see on your journey towards freedom, a dopamine detox will provide you with many other tools worth fighting for.

Teaches Discipline and Freedom

Although discipline and independence are two characteristics that seem to contradict each other, they are also closely linked. In fact, the more disciplined someone is, the more freedom they possess. When we go through dopamine detox, we distance ourselves from everything that takes away our willpower. As a result of this, our self-control grows again - especially if we also participate in mindfulness activities.

The core of this solution lies in delaying instant gratification, which we can only learn if our mind is free of high doses of dopamine. Then we comprehend that by not giving in right away, we can develop a higher form of self-discipline called willpower. That said, this inner strength is not something we are born with, nor can we maintain it without exercising it from time to time. Just like muscles, willpower grows stronger with training. But to train it, we must liberate it first through a dopamine detox.

Having done that, we become free to choose how to be stronger. The method will depend on our abilities, preferences, and several other influences that this detox uncovers. Even the smallest act of self-discipline represents a challenge for someone with dopamine addiction. Having to resist giving in to instant gratification can lead to willpower depletion, which will be discussed in one of the following chapters. But if we manage to surpass that, our freedom will become even greater, not to mention cherished.

Expands Our Comfort Zone

Comfort zones are all about what feels familiar - and by extension, safe. For example, it's much safer to return to addictive behaviors reinforced by dopamine than pursue new experiences. However, continuing with this addictive behavior narrows our thinking and causes us to get stuck in our tiny comfort zone. Despite suffering the emotional and physical consequences of this narrow thought process, we're often unable to acknowledge that the reason we can't step out of this zone lies in our addiction. Instead, we choose the safer path. We mask our feelings and thoughts by seeking the same pleasures again, looking for that dopamine shot.

Dopamine detox breaks our addictions to comfort, allowing us to have new experiences. This causes our comfort zone to expand naturally, and the bigger it becomes, the more confidence we gain. We soon begin to accept that many new things we thought to be miles away from our comfort zone are actually just a few steps beyond it. As scary as it sounds, the best things in life are just outside of this area.

The things we can experience beyond our comfort zone are often surprising but in a good way. They teach us new lessons, help us grow and become open to new ideas and situations, and ultimately have a great time. They show us that we must pursue our goals and responsibilities instead of being complacent.

Improves Focus

As we distance ourselves from our dopamine triggers, our general focus improves. We can concentrate on accomplishing more tasks throughout the day and can approach them in smarter ways. For example, most people are more productive during the first half of the day, but their focus slowly depletes as the hours go by. This is also related to decision fatigue, and it often results in poor decisions made in the second half of the day. Over time, this leads to severe addiction and the tendency to make poor choices at all times because our brains become so overworked we feel a constant need for a dopamine hit.

However, when we detox, our brain to go without dopamine hits. The more successful we become at the detox, the more we show ourselves that we can perform without receiving some type of gratification at all times. This further promotes the elimination of distractions and temptations altogether. As a result, we have enough time to accomplish the more complex tasks earlier in the day.

Our brain doesn't have to get overworked, and there will be less chance of making poor decisions. Suddenly we can focus on day-to-day tasks, relationships, health, environment, and much more. It's a far better solution than any other stimulant that promises to help with the stress of a busy schedule.

Provides Motivation

Despite our highly developed minds being capable of handling a myriad of processes at once, dopamine forces us to act irrationally. Because of this, we engage in unproductive behavior, becoming hooked on dangerous vices, which overpower our intrinsic self-motivational tools. While it seems that we draw inspiration from the pleasurable activities we partake in, this isn't a true motivation. To overcome this, we need our minds to be dopamine-free to focus on what we can achieve instead of this false sense of motivation.

As our focus improves, we notice that we are suddenly much more productive throughout the day. Unlike dopamine which gives pleasure without context, the satisfaction following each fulfilled responsibility is real and long-lasting. This inspires us to take on more tasks on a professional level - to gain new skills and improve our financial security.

Moreover, our dopamine-free brain motivates us to set up new goals in our personal life. Without constant distractions from the pleasure center of our brains, we're able to work towards these and become motivated enough to grow as an individual. Because while we all know life is hard, and there are things we should fear, if we have true motivation, we can overcome all our fears and obstacles in life.

Relaxes the Mind

Since we can focus on accomplishing more tasks earlier in the day, this leaves us with more space for contemplation. After all, how often do we have time to reflect on our choices, get immersed in our present, or wonder what lies beyond it? We rarely ever do this anymore. We live busy lives, and whenever we have even the smallest bit of free time, we reach for the tool that gives us the dopamine hit and distracts us from these questions.

With all the stimuli we receive from various sources, there is no wonder our minds can't relax enough to contemplate anything meaningful. It's too busy taking in content from social platforms and all the other media we are bombarded with. And while we know that the content isn't always positive, we still crave it to get the dopamine release that follows. We all also know that we shouldn't use these dopamine shots as crutches, but we can't seem to help ourselves.

By removing the tools that give this release, we can finally think about anything we want to. We can do this while waiting in line or sitting in the park during lunch hour - the time we would usually spend seeking out the dopamine-inducing pleasure of our choice. A dopamine detox gives us back this time for ourselves, when we can focus on what we want from our present and future life, what we can put into the world, and much more.

Helps Set Up Goals

Due to our fast-paced culture, we have been taught to think only about short-term goals. After all, this is one of the main reasons we become addicted to instant gratification in the first place. We can conquer this paradigm through mindfulness exercises and other dopamine detox techniques. Around the same time, we notice that we can focus and be productive; we also learn that patience is a highly esteemed virtue that comes with many advantages.

Setting short-term objectives is a great start for boosting your productivity. However, achieving these makes us more confident in establishing long-term goals. In turn, these bring a lot more satisfaction and a much greater sense of fulfillment - in whichever area of life they might come. Without distractions and anxiety looming over our shoulders, we become aware of what we're capable of accomplishing.

On the other hand, we must keep in mind that such benefits only come from a healthy release of dopamine detox. Otherwise, we might end up eliminating all sources of pleasure in our lives - which once again causes the loss of productivity and unhappiness. If we manage to find a way to seek out short happiness in a healthier way, we will be much more likely to take action to improve our lives in the long run.

Increases Creativity

When we spend our time focusing on the source of dopamine release (such as social media and other addictive pleasure-inducing tools), we can only work towards getting this and not much else. And since we know we only get the shot if we act in a certain way, we don't feel the need to engage in any creative thinking process. After all, we don't need a vision if we are just devouring. When in fact, this couldn't be further from the truth. For our imagination could be our greatest strength.

Apart from contemplating choices and goals, being alone allows us to dream, imagine, think, and ultimately achieve great things in life. But for this, we must give our brain time to establish itself instead of ingesting content from the dopamine release source. Dopamine detox brings back this amazing ability, even if it's hard to believe it can be possible again.

Some people aren't even aware of what their creative side is capable of until they tap into it by taking a different approach on a difficult assignment or starting a new hobby. A dopamine-free mind allows us to re-evaluate our moments of solitude. Instead of looking at them as a source of discomfort, use them to come up with new ideas or find new perspectives for the old ones.

Improves Our Mood

For those familiar with spirituality, it is no surprise that we also attract positive energy when we are in a higher vibrational state. While this is often linked to health benefits, the vibrations can affect much more than that - at least when it comes to the dopamine loop. Even if we are lucky enough to avoid mental health issues, our dopamine levels' constant highs and lows can drastically affect our mood.

To improve our mood, we often reach for the tool that stimulates the part of our brain capable of granting instant dopamine release. However, since this release stops immediately after achieving instant gratification, the levels of dopamine in our body plummet, causing our mood to follow as well. So, we seek the source that leads to this empty release once again, continuing this vicious cycle.

The only way out of this is through a dopamine detox. While challenging, this process grants us the ability to stabilize our mood in the long run, allowing us to make some constructive changes in our lives. After all, what better way to improve our mood than to see our goals realized after plenty of productive days - the days we would have wasted on engaging in pleasure-seeking activities, not for the detox.

Tames Unhealthy Desires

Dopamine is just one of those chemicals that compels us to come back for it, no matter how many times we have been through its loop. It makes this dopamine-induced pleasure really difficult to avoid, to the extent that eventually we can't avoid it at all, and we become devoured by this compulsion. Whatever advantage we think we gain from it will disappear soon after the release, leaving behind a void even greater than it was before.

A dopamine detox removes the sources of these desires, liberating us from the wants that have controlled our everyday life. It also improves emotional regulation as now we are forced to re-evaluate our emotions. As we stay away from those toxic sources of pleasure, our emotional life becomes more regulated, peaceful, and, most importantly, pain-free.

This detox improves our ability to resist temptation rooted in those guilty pleasures that hooked us on this dopamine cycle. The next time we are tempted to reach for the same dopamine-inducing tool, we will be able to stop and consider whether we really need that shot or we can find pleasure in simpler things in life. Sooner or later, we learn that we only need to make positive choices to have a fulfilling life. These are often harder than we are used to making, but they offer far bigger rewards willing to take them on.

Increases Satisfaction Levels

Without having a peaceful and overall fulfilled life, we can't expect to be satisfied with it either. More often than not, life satisfaction is linked to our comfort zone. However, another aspect of dopamine detox also affects how we can reach the optimal level of being pleased with our choices and life in general. By taking away our fears and other stress factors, dopamine detox brings us back to a state of bliss where everything seems more positive.

One of the perks of having a dopamine-free mind is looking back at past actions, clearly seeing their consequences, and learning from them. So, when we look back at a negative experience, we can think about the lessons they taught us rather than the pain they have caused. Because just as it isn't feasible to eliminate all the pleasurable experiences from our life, it's not possible to do with the negative ones either.

In this day and age, when there are so many temptations that threaten to distract us and cause us grief in more ways than one, the only way to triumph in life is to find a balance through a dopamine detox. It's a process that enables us to consciously abstain from behaviors that have the potential to get out of our control. At the same time, it grants access to long-term goals that bring forth the ultimate satisfaction one can achieve.

Promotes Healthier Relationships

We are taught new patterns of socially accepted behavior on an ongoing basis - but not all of them are good for us. Nevertheless, the dopamine release from the acknowledgment we receive when we adopt these behaviors creates a false sense of happiness and a broad range of unhealthy relationships. The lack of response and dopamine release can hit hard at first, but soon we learn the error we were making in relationships that matter.

Whatever type of addictive behavior you are struggling with, social media can contribute to it. Dismissing it from your life, even for a little bit, will allow you to see its true effects, which will result in building a healthier relationship with yourself. Breaking the pattern of compulsive behaviors will ignite the desire to change much more than our relationships with digital technology or social media. Achieving this is a good stepping stone when learning to understand addiction.

However, to build a better life, we must establish a healthier relationship with our environment as well - and this is when dopamine detox comes in handy. Ever noticed that when you pay more attention to your emotions, you're able to communicate them better? This is not a coincidence. When we aren't distracted by compulsive behavior, we can focus on our relationships with those around us. As these people notice our interest in them (instead of being lost in our own world), they will reciprocate, and much deeper bonds will form.

Improves Mental and Physical Health

Taking the extra step to achieve all these goals reflects our increased ability to solve potentially problematic behaviors. The roots of all our negative behavioral patterns lie in a poor mental state caused by our dopamine addictions. Therefore, removing the constant boost of high doses of this hormone can examine our minds, improve our thought processes, and feel better in general. Our state of mind often affects the health of our bodies - and now we may have overcome potential health issues as well.

Without a screen, substance, or anything else to distract us, we become much more aware of ourselves. This may sound terrifying to some initially, causing a sudden mental block. However, with enough determination and motivation, everyone can move past this hindrance and enjoy the freedom of their mind and body.

As we improve our mental and physical health, we will sense our spiritual energy (vibe or vibration) being lifted. Due to the numerous distractions, our vibrational energy can get off-balance, leading to many issues this book has already discussed. When we get out of that constant dopamine loop, we can boost our vibe and attract more positive and productive energy into our lives. Suddenly, we start to notice the positive changes the healthier habits are bringing - and it's all because our brain isn't bombarded with this addictive molecule anymore.

Key Takeaways

- If performed the healthy way, a dopamine detox is beneficial, even if most of them last for short periods at a time.

- Long term-benefits are also possible, but they require a lot of effort and time to achieve. To obtain them, we must arm ourselves with patience.

- The first and most notable advantage of dopamine detox lies in the paradox of discipline providing freedom. The more we discipline ourselves, the more liberty we gain to do whatever we want in life.

- We gain the ability to liberate ourselves from an unhealthy culture of distractions.

- The lack of dopamine production teaches us that giving in to desires is not always a good idea. Sometimes, taming our passions is necessary before they devour us completely.

- Staying away from triggers allows our mind to focus on the present activities and our physical and spiritual wellbeing.

- Since we aren't bombarded with constant dopamine release anymore, we can pay more attention to our energy (or vibe) and sense its natural elevation.

- Away from the distractions, we discover how to contemplate various aspects of our lives, which allows us to change anything we need to.

- With an improved focus, we become motivated to achieve more in life and become productive members of our society. We learn to establish short and long-term goals.

- With a lot more free time on our hands, we can also explore our creativity and even find new hobbies or career paths.

- The inability to enjoy certain pleasures will drive us to explore new ones. While this often pushes us out of our comfort zone, it also teaches us to enjoy new things.

- By denying ourselves instant gratification, we learn about greater pleasures in life, such as the importance of building healthier relationships with our environment.

- Since our brain continues to produce dopamine in smaller increments, detoxing from it requires a rather specific approach. You will learn how to fully detox your brain's dopamine production from the next chapter.

6

Detox Your Brain

In the previous chapters, we explored the idea of addiction and discussed dopamine fasting as a viable way to break this harmful cycle. However, up until this point, you may still have your doubts. How can you effectively let go of the things that trigger those dopamine spikes and give you instant contentment? Make no mistake, it will be a very tough journey, and it doesn't help that the digital world is ideally specifically organized to exploit our dopamine systems either deliberately or by chance. However, with dedication, motivation, and the right strategies, you will be able to replace those harmful habits with healthier ones.

Many of the most common addictions, along with increased rates of depression, anxiety, and other mental health issues prevalent in society, are reinforced by modern technology. Life today is incredibly stressful and fast-paced, which forces us to resort to cheap and easily accessible doses of dopamine. Before we know it, society becomes dependent on these happiness and temporary escapism methods.

As you already know, a dopamine detox can help you get rid of your unhealthy addictions as it realigns your mind. This happens when you train yourself to adopt new, healthy, and fulfilling habits. This way, you replace the pleasure you felt from addictive behaviors with the pleasure you can get from new habits, activities, and experiences. An added advantage is that your new ventures will give you longer-lasting contentment, rather than the "quick fix" dopamine hit you were a slave to in the past. This chapter explains how dopamine detox works and provides tips and rules that will help you succeed in your journey. It also gives you numerous helpful techniques and strategies that you can use to leave your unwanted habits behind.

How It Works

One thing that you need to keep in mind as you embark on your "dopamine detox" journey is that there is no one correct way to go about it. There are numerous approaches you can take, depending on various personal factors. Each person's journey is different, and we all respond differently to the same things. This means that what works for someone else may not necessarily work for you. Finding the right technique for you could need a lot of introspection and experimentation on your part. However, there's no need to worry because we're here to help you out. But before we look into the different strategies you can use, we need to explain how they work.

Since the behaviors you're struggling to get rid of are repetitive, we can describe them as "loops." In other words, any behavior loop is a cycle where the person experiences a trigger responds with a certain action, which triggers a response. When the response is favorable, like a dopamine hit, this action is reinforced in your case. There are generally two types of loops: escape loops and engagement loops.

Unwanted Behaviors: Escape Loops

An escape loop consists of anything or any behavior in your life that offers you low-value contentment or pleasure. These loops are distinguished by the significant, quick, cheap, and easy hits of dopamine that they offer. A typical escape loop may look something like the following:

You experience negative emotions like sadness, anxiety, boredom, or loneliness. This emotion leaves you feeling unfulfilled or unsatisfied. It is accompanied by low-level stress and stimulates a rise in cortisol levels. Naturally, you feel compelled to change the uncomfortable feelings, and you resort to one of two options: identifying the root of the problem and fixing it, which is often a long and more difficult solution, or finding a cheaper, quicker, and more accessible escape to trigger a spike in your dopamine levels.

You feel ecstatic after you indulge in this "escape" or behavior. When you feel triggered again, you decide to do it once more because a few times can't hurt, right? Your brain tricks you into believing that you're in control of the situation. But sooner or later, you can't help but rely on this action for that period of extreme pleasure. Before you know it, you're stuck in a dependent feedback loop.

Escape loops provide a way (a very unhealthy one) to maneuver around the primary cause of the problem. Instead of having to go to all the trouble of fixing the problem so you can feel better, this escape plan allows you to just skip to finding instant relief and contentment. Even if this pleasure is shallow, and even when you know it's wrong, finding a quick way out would sound appealing to just about anyone. The problem is, not only is this behavior is very detrimental for your social, psychological, spiritual, and physical well-being in the long run, but it also leaves you feeling horrible after you've experienced that momentary hit of pleasure. It's a self-destructive loop.

Instead of taking up a hobby, most people pick up their phones whenever boredom strikes. Those who don't like their jobs drown their sorrows each night instead of searching for a new job opportunity. People who feel lonely may end up watching porn to fill that temporary void, so they don't risk having to sit through a few "bad" dates. Each person's escape loop is different, but they're all destructive.

So, what's the solution?

Replacing Unwanted Behaviors: Engagement Loops

As you can tell, an engagement loop is basically the opposite of an escape loop. Instead of allowing yourself to indulge in those quick sources of dopamine, you force yourself to delay the pleasure you so you can create richer and more meaningful life experiences for yourself. If you don't make this decision a conscious one, you let yourself fall into the traps that the digital age has created for us.

As we mentioned above, not indulging in an engagement loop is typically the harder, more taxing choice, especially when you have an addiction to let go of. These engaging behaviors are the things that everyone knows they need to do yet don't wish to do them. It only makes sense that after a long day, you wouldn't want to hit the gym, go for a run, meet people, or go hobby hunting instead of resorting to your comfort zone.

At times you feel that partaking in this harmful behavior is not that much of an issue. You scroll through your feed for a few minutes before your friends arrive or have just one drink on a night out. However, unfortunately, it doesn't always work that way. No matter how small it is, every action serves as a foundation for the life you're building for yourself. Good actions and smart, conscious choices will give you a good and healthy life. Harmful ones (especially those you're already struggling with) will just stand in the way of the future you're trying to create.

We've already taken a look at the typical escape loop. So, what does an engagement loop look like?

You start to experience negative feelings, like sadness, anxiety, boredom, or loneliness. This feeling leaves you unfulfilled and comes with low-level stress. Again, it stimulates a rise in cortisol levels, and you feel the need to resolve the situation by resorting to one of either options.This time, instead of going for the easy fix, you decide to delve deep into the root cause of the problem. This means that you're willing to walk the tough path of fixing it. After you do some deep reflection and perhaps participate in any fulfilling and enriching activities, you will start to feel a lot better about yourself and your decisions. The unparalleled sense of accomplishment, along with the joy that your newly-adopted hobbies give you then positively reinforced every time you consciously make a positive decision.

Engagement loops are very hard to sustain. They require ongoing effort, dedication, motivation, willpower, and hard work. However, once established, they provide a profound feeling of fulfillment and meaning. They provide you with the chance to create lasting change in your life and give you the chance to redefine your purpose. Like escape loops, each person has a different engagement loop. This is why you need to find a method or activity that works for you to sustain this loop in the long run. Examples of engagement loops include disconnecting from the digital world, connecting with others in person, reading, dating, eating a healthy diet, and physical activity.

Establishing an Engagement Loop

To establish an engagement loop, you need to do a little introspection. You need to find out why you're feeling that way, to begin with. Then, identify your go-to behaviors or escapes. Is there something in particular that can be fixed? Does this type of behavior link back to a psychological issue, trauma, or something in your past history? In other words, is there a reason why you developed this particular habit in the first place? Think about where you're avoiding responsibility and how your future self will be affected by your current actions. Think about your goals and what you can do to either move toward or away from these goals.

Consider the challenges that you usually encounter in life. Think about your shortcomings and past failures and how you can become a better person. Take the time to reflect on all these things and how they may have impacted how you deal with obstacles. Identify the root causes, face them, and accept them, as these are the things that you need to challenge throughout your journey. The answers you come up with are essentially things you don't want to deal with and therefore seek an escape loop.

If you have more than one escape strategy, focus on one at a time. However, you don't need to stick to one engagement loop for each undesirable behavior. You may find a collection of positive engagements to be the most effective, as they would provide you with large amounts of dopamine over a short amount of time. The more layered engagement loops you have, the more likely you will stick to these lifestyle changes.

Visualize Your Future

Take as much time as you need to visualize yourself 5, 10, or even 15 years from now. Write down everything that comes to your mind. Visualize yourself down to the smallest detail.

Envision your home, how it's furnished and decorated, what you look like, how you dress, your car, and whether you have a family. If you have a family of your own, think about your relationship with them and how you interact with each other. Visualize the time you spend with them and the activities you do together. Think about your job. Where do you work? What does your office look like? What does your typical day at work look like? Think about your eating habits. Are you vegan? Are you eating a balanced diet? Perhaps you go to the gym, and you're bulking. What activities do you do? Are you taking them professionally? Do you have any pets? Do you travel regularly?

Now that you know what you want your future to look like, think about your life right now. What steps do you need to take to pursue this future? Will your escape loop help you get there? If not, how will it stand in your way? What does the perfect engagement loop look like? What activities and type of lifestyle will help you get there? This is not supposed to make you feel pressured at all. You don't need to make these changes overnight. That would be impossible. The small steps and the whole journey are what matter. Turn to your ideal, future self whenever you need the motivation to move forward.

Detoxing

There isn't a certain set of rigid rules that you need to follow on your dopamine detox. This typically depends on how long you plan to do it. A deep detox that allows you to cut off all your bad habits would be ideal. However, many people prefer to detox their brains for a certain period of time first. Keep in mind that the following 24-hour and 30-day detoxes are designed to tackle several aspects of your life rather than one specific escape loop. Temporary lifestyle changes will not prevent you from falling into the same traps and facing the same problems in the long run, either.

The 24-hour detox is very challenging and is therefore not sustainable in any way. It will leave you with a very minimal impact unless you do a follow-up detox plan. Many people find it hard to implement all the rules of the 30-day detox into their long-term lifestyle, as well.

You can do these detoxes to reset your brain and fully detox its dopamine production before dealing with your escape loops and making permanent lifestyle changes.

24-Hour Dopamine Detox

You should do this detox on the weekend or while you're on vacation. If you want, you can inform your friends and family that you will not be able to get in touch with them for the following 24 hours. Here are the rules you need to follow:

- Don't use any electronics, including your phone, computer, and TV.

- Don't read magazines, books, or newspapers.

- Don't talk.

- Don't have sex or masturbate.

- Don't eat. If you have a health condition, you need to consult your doctor first. Drinking water is allowed, of course.

- Don't drink coffee or consume other stimulants.

- Don't listen to music or podcasts.

- Don't watch movies, videos, or TV.

Translate Your Escape Loops into Engagement Loops

It's not feasible to run off to a secluded place and lead the life of a monk for months on end (if this sounds like something you can do, then lucky you!). All jokes aside, taking a measured approach that accounts for modern-day responsibilities and dynamics would be more effective anyway. The 30-day detox and the strategies we'll discuss will allow you to operate and partake in society.

As you know, you need to gradually introduce positive habits into your life to get rid of negative ones. Determine which escape loop is most problematic and takes the largest toll on your dopamine system. Match this escape loop with at least three engagement loops you can potentially replace it with. The examples and things that you need to reflect on, as mentioned above, can help you pinpoint your burden, its impact on your life, and how you can positively approach it. For instance: if you feel lonely and bored, and spend all your time on dating apps, go out and date traditionally and intentionally. Whenever you feel unlucky and tempted to match with people on dating apps, go outside for a walk or engage in a fulfilling activity (more on that later).

Your positive loops should be somewhat associated with the negative ones. It helps translate the escape loop you're struggling with into an equivalent engagement strategy. For instance: if you can't stay away from social media, then you need to experience more in-person connections. If you watch pornography, you need to find meaningful intimacy. If you can't stop checking your mobile notifications, you need to take some time to disconnect every day. The healthy equivalent of over-indulging in junk food would be eating healthier. Those who can't stop using dating apps need to replace this with intentional dating. Video-game addicts need to read more books.

You need to understand the main cause behind your discontentment and why you're seeking those quick fixes so you can come up with a related, healthier alternative. The key here is to train your mind to immediately detect when you're turning to your unhealthy behaviors. This way, you can break the chain before it begins by heading for your engagement loop instead. Doing so will slowly disincentivize your escape behaviors. At the same time, it will establish a positive feedback loop for your healthy ones. Your engagement loop is specific to you and should be tailored to your needs and lifestyle, which is why you should think deeply about the behaviors you should apply.

30-Day Dopamine Detox

Here are some rules and tips that you can follow on your 30-day (or longer) dopamine detox:

- Turn off all your phone's push notifications and badge icons.

- Put your phone on silent or "do not disturb."

- Uninstall all dating, work-related, and social media apps from your phone.

- Turn off your notifications and stop checking your emails (unless they're related to work) when you're working.

- Always avoid multi-tasking. Focus on one task at a time.

- Spend some time outdoors every day.

- Meditate daily. Even a few minutes will suffice.

- Spend time with your friends, significant other, and family. Don't use your phone when you're with them.

- Try journaling.

- Drink a lot of water every day.

Keep in mind that these are just a few suggestions. If you decide to stick to this detox as it is, keep note of the things that seem to work for you and the things that don't. This will help you find out which changes work and that you can sustain in the long term. Another option would be tweaking these suggestions so they suit your needs. This way, you can stick to these "rules" instead of regarding it as a 30-day challenge.

Let's take a look at some of the techniques and strategies that you can incorporate into your lifestyle.

Techniques and Strategies

These strategies and techniques work as great engagement loops to replace your negative habits. You may find some of them unappealing at first. However, we encourage you to try them out before dismissing them right away.

Daily Meditation

Meditation is a practice that has long been proven to improve one's overall quality of life. It promotes calmness and serenity and allows you to deal with triggers positively. This is why it can be a great engagement technique and can be used as a long-term dopamine detox strategy. You may be surprised to learn that many rehabilitation centers regard meditation as a very valuable therapy technique, which is why they incorporate it into their holistic treatment plans. This activity works by forging a mind-body connection to stimulate a state of relaxation.

When you're meditating, you need to sit somewhere quiet to regulate your attention. The idea behind this practice is to let your thoughts flow through your mind without examining the distractions. Practitioners usually pair meditation with deep breathing exercises to boost their focus.

Daily stressors and experiences, especially those that trigger anxiety, excessive stress, boredom, sadness, and other negative emotions, can make it very hard to avoid seeking quick dopamine hits. Mindful meditation, however, is proven to reduce these types of symptoms. This relieves the need to reach for an escape loop. Additionally, the more you practice meditation, the more effectively you'll be able to control your responses. This means that it will provide you with skills that will benefit you for life.

Making meditation a part of your daily routine will help you in your dopamine detox journey regardless of where you are. There are several ways in which you can incorporate it into your lifestyle. For instance, you can join a meditation or yoga class, practice deep breathing, pray, or take long relaxing walks in nature. Take the time to notice your bodily sensations every day and make it a habit to focus on positive emotions like gratitude, joy, and love.

Breathing Techniques

Breathing impacts our life experiences to the point where changing our breathing patterns can give us more or less control over them. Our brain chemistry is also affected by our breathing, and therefore it impacts our emotions and mood.

Doing breathing exercises or techniques can help relax our muscles and lower blood pressure, which, in turn, will improve the way that we respond to external stressors. These techniques can also stimulate the production of feel-good chemicals in the brain, reducing the need to resort to an instant dopamine fix.

Relaxation is among the most noticeable effects that deep breathing haves on us. This is because the process facilitates more oxygen being delivered to the muscles, which releases built-up tension. When this tension is released, we feel a lot more relaxed. The fact that these techniques help uplift our mood by influencing the levels of neurotransmitters in the brain also makes them great engagement tactics. Our neurotransmitters are responsible for transporting emotions and thoughts.

Here are some examples of breathing exercises that you can try out:

Stimulating Breath

1. Close your eyes and relax your jaw.

2. Set a timer.

3. Inhale and exhale quickly through your nose.

4. Check if you were able to get three breaths in and out in just one second

5. Do that for 15 seconds.

6. Keep increasing the time until you reach one minute.

Breath Counting

1. Bring your attention to your breath as you stay quiet for a few minutes.

2. Start counting once you bring awareness to your inhalation and exhalation rhythm.

3. Count "one" on your first exhale, then "two" on the other exhale.

4. Keep counting your exhales until you reach the fifth one, and then start all over again.

5. Don't control your breathing pattern or rhythm in the process. Let it flow naturally.

4-7-8 Breathing

1. Exhale fully.

2. Inhale through your nose for four counts.

3. Hold your breath for seven counts.

4. Exhale as you count to eight.

5. Repeat the steps four times.

Cold Showers

You may be surprised to learn that cold water Hydrotherapy–bathing was prescribed to treat a wide array of ailments. In the 1930s, this type of therapy was also first used to treat addiction. The benefits of cold water have been recently re-explored, and the treatment is believed to help with anxiety, depression, sleep, and the enhancement of the immune system.

When you shower under cold water, noradrenaline levels rise, which is the fight or flight hormone. Getting your body to believe that you're in danger will undoubtedly override your initial negative emotions. It also works by driving more blood toward your brain and other major organs, improving their function. Cold showers can also reduce brain inflammations associated with depression and other negative feelings.

While noradrenaline is linked to panic, cold showers can help with anxiety. This is because they also trigger a rise in beta-endorphin levels. This performs the same function as opioid drugs, suppressing the opioid receptors. These endorphins can help reduce stress and improve your overall homeostasis. The most important aspects of better homeostasis include behavioral stability and gratification.

Practicing Mindfulness

Mindfulness can help you feel better because it lets you take a moment to slow everything down. This includes racing around in either your thoughts or activities. In other words, it can keep you from getting over-stimulated. This technique can help you take control of your thoughts and mental conversations. This way, you can take a moment or two to think about whether your escape cycle is worth reaching out to before you indulge in any negative behaviors. Mindfulness can give you the sense of calm and tranquility that you seek from these undesirable actions.

Mindfulness techniques open your eyes to small details that you've never noticed before. In the process, you'll encounter sensory experiences that you've never had the chance to pay attention to before. Once you get in the zone, you will not actively try to leave that state of consciousness and seek addictive behaviors. The more you practice, the deeper you'll understand how you react to things. You will find it easier to let go of thoughts and feelings that hold you back and trigger your escape loop.

There are six key things that mindfulness can help you achieve:

1. **Observation:** Directing your awareness to the world around you.

2. **Description:** Practicing your ability to describe, in full detail, your experiences and how you felt as they happened.

3. **Participation:** Partaking in activities without feeling self-conscious.

4. **Being Non-Judgmental:** Accepting things the way they are rather than judging them.

5. **One Thing at a Time:** Avoiding multi-tasking and handling one thing at a time without allowing any internal or external distractions to interfere.

6. **Effectiveness:** Doing things effectively without doubting your abilities.

Exercising and Sports

Physical activity can help you find a way out of your escape loop by providing a positive outlet for your feelings. When you leave your stress levels unmanaged, you are likely to resort to harmful behaviors. Fortunately, sports can help reduce cortisol levels, a stress-related hormone. Strenuous activity also promotes the production of endorphins and gets your blood circulating properly. Exercise can lift your mood and increase your overall energy level. Taking part in physical activity can keep you from returning to your bad habits by helping with trigger management.

Journaling

Writing down all your thoughts and feelings can be of great help throughout your dopamine detox journey. It can help you stay motivated as you track your progress, serving as a source of self-realization and, of course, expression. Journaling can help you curb your triggers as it aids with anxiety and stress relief. It also promotes a sense of accomplishment, inner peace, and emotional awareness. Journaling can help you stay on track by allowing you to focus on your goals and helping you see things from a different point of view. There are numerous types of journals that you can keep, depending on your preferences: reflection journal, diary, gratitude journal, health journal (if you're trying to break free of bingeing cycles, substance abuse, or alcoholic tendencies), or a journal for your goal.

Socializing and Staying Active

The most important thing you need to do when it comes to leaving unhelpful habits behind is by asking yourself how you can make better use of your time. Make a list of activities you feel you may be interested in doing whenever you get bored. Since we typically don't have much time to think before we act impulsively (or reach to escape loops), it helps to keep this list somewhere visible. The activities should be easy and accessible, such as cleaning up, reading, drawing, painting, dancing, cycling, or running.

You should also aim to dedicate some of your time to socializing with your friends and family and learning new skills. Make self-development and growth a priority. Try to spend at least 10 minutes every day outside. You can use this as an opportunity to empty your mind and connect with nature. Your dopamine detox is the perfect chance to do anything (positive) that you've always wanted to do but never had the chance or courage to.

Digesting Long-Form Content

Indulging in mindless and unproductive activities is one reason you always go back to your escape cycle. At the same time, mindful activities can get very tiring to keep up. Ideally, you should seek out long-form content because it's qualitative and can be digested slowly. For instance, you can read or listen to audiobooks or play board games with your friends. You can watch a movie as long as you don't use your phone, or other things, as a distraction. You can also listen attentively to music and not just leave it to play aimlessly in the background. When consuming long-form content, you're less likely to be compulsive.

In this chapter, we have discussed:

- An escape loop consists of anything or any behavior in your life that offers you low-value contentment or pleasure.

- These loops are quick, affordable, and provide instant pleasure.

- To fully detox your brain's dopamine production, you need to translate your escape loops into their counter engagement loops.

- You can try a 24-hour or 30-day detox before making permanent lifestyle changes.

- Daily meditation, breathing techniques, cold showers, practicing mindfulness. Exercising and doing sports, journaling, socializing, staying active, and digesting long-form content are among the techniques you can use to let go of your escape loops.

7

Overcoming Relapse

As you have seen from the previous chapter, there are several techniques that you can use to t overcoming dopamine addiction. However, sometimes the cravings and the withdrawal symptoms are too strong for the brain to stop the addictive behavior. As the behavior continues to stimulate dopamine production and our brain gets more rewarding pleasure, this system truly acts against our benefit. Not only does this leave our body continually in need of more, but the psychological effects often remain for months or even years after the physical dependency is gone.

This intense desire to reach for the "reward" in recovery often leads to physical symptoms. Our brain can recall the emotions caused by dopamine release, which can activate the production of dopamine even without the trigger actually being present in our lives. Desperate to feel this pleasure once more, the brain produces withdrawal symptoms.

This dopamine relapse can lead us right back to the beginning and to us engaging in addictive behavior again. Since this occurs in response to emotional triggers (such as stress and anxiety), being aware of dopamine's role in our risk of relapse is a powerful recovery tool. From this chapter, you will learn what it takes to successfully complete a dopamine fasting phase and avoid or overcome dopamine relapse.

Recognizing Triggers

Knowing what may trigger a dopamine relapse is essential for avoiding it and helps overcome it. It's a good idea to do a quick mental sweep to reveal your triggers. This analysis starts with the social environment - the people we associate with the addictive behavior. Then we move on to uncovering places and items that remind us of the source of addiction one by one. Keep in mind that most triggers are closely connected with the source by either time or physical proximity.

But since triggers aren't only people, items, or places, we can't limit our mental search to these things. For example, major sources of stress can also act in the same way. Being overwhelmed can make anyone feel that they can't deal with their issues, avoiding them through addictive behavior.

Habits have a similar effect. For example, if we used to come home, sit down, and start spending time with our vices, following the same pattern without being triggered will be challenging. Apart from the free time now we have at our hands, our brain may turn to other "substitutional" feelings such as hunger, anger, tiredness, or loneliness - none of which may be real, but they can trigger a relapse.

Avoiding triggers is the best way to decrease the likelihood of a dopamine relapse. That said, the busy world we live in makes it impossible to avoid all the triggers. So, the next best thing we can do is recognize what leads us to impulse and addictive behaviors. Working against these takes an enormous amount of patience - but the freedom we gain from being dopamine free is definitely worth it. Nothing can beat the feeling of satisfaction you gain from sources that don't depend on anything but your own will.

Being Ready for Surprises

No matter how well you plan your recovery journey, there will always be surprises. Triggers come from unexpected places at unexpected times, and we must be ready to deal with them. The best way to do this is to have a backup plan. Having someone to talk to in emergency situations can also do the trick. Still, we must learn how to cope with triggers by ourselves for long-term success. Developing strategies to calm ourselves will be much more effective as they will help us remember that all emotions are transitory, including the cravings for dopamine. Additionally, being aware of possible negative emotions will allow us to deal with them effectively, even if they take us by surprise. Here are some tips for dealing with your feelings during a dopamine fasting phase.

Know What Makes You Uncomfortable

More often than not, addictive patterns are developed because of our efforts to avoid uncomfortable feelings. And these feelings will arise during the fasting phase too. We can suddenly find ourselves in a situation where we feel self-conscious, bored, or even anxious. Before we know it, our brain signals us the need for a dopamine release.

Since we have been taken by surprise, these emotions can hit even more powerfully, intensifying the craving even more. Learning to resist them regardless of their intensity will allow us to manage addictive behaviors during and after the fasting phase. A broad range of mindfulness exercises is designed to analyze negative emotions and accept them without judgment.

Don't Act Impulsively

Following impulses is never a good idea during dopamine fasting, much less acting upon them. That said, some experiences can wake them up without warning, and you must be ready for them. The cravings, the desire to fulfill them, and the impulse to act on them are typical in dopamine relapse. Suppressing the instinctive movement to reach for a source of pleasure is the second most challenging part of a recovery journey, right after the changes in lifestyle and environment.

Fortunately, there is always a possibility to slow this movement down and even reverse it if necessary. We can reach a state of mind where we're able to avoid getting pulled back into a dopamine loop, despite the intense craving that precedes our impulse to act. Practicing this takes a lot of time and effort, but we can become self-aware over time, and our ability to control our impulses will improve. Keep in mind that impulses coming from different sources often lead to the same reaction. This means that learning to suppress instinctive behavior in one field won't be enough. You will need to do this with all the possible trigger sources.

Take Time for Yourself

The last step we can take to prepare ourselves for surprises is simply to make time for ourselves. This has two main purposes, and one of these is to take us away from trigger sources in the first place. After all, if you are far away from what caused your dopamine addiction, you will be less likely to suffer a relapse. The second purpose of this exercise is to give yourself enough time to go through what was discussed in the previous steps. Being away from the distractions will let your mind relax and contemplate all your emotions so you can plan for surprise triggers.

Preparing for a Long Journey

Many people in recovery don't realize that a short period of dopamine fasting often isn't enough to eliminate addictive behavior. So, if you thought that doing dopamine fasting for a day would cure you of your addiction, you are wrong. It takes time to build up the reward-seeking behavior, so it makes sense that a short detox will not be enough to eliminate it either.

Not only that, but jumping right in and eliminating all the triggers at once will make a dopamine relapse more likely. A better solution is to go through the fasting phase slowly and without taking drastic measures to speed things up. Taking the long road will make it easier to obtain sustainable results.

In addition, the sense of clarity we get from a short fasting phase will most likely only be a placebo. While our brain's ability to recover is astounding, it still needs time to learn new patterns and leave the old ones behind. Depending on the severity of your addiction, it may take months and years to recover fully.

Unfortunately, this is one of the reasons why many people opt-out from dopamine fasting in the first place. But if you are serious about your recovery, you must prepare yourself for a long and challenging journey. There will be lots of temptation along the way, but the perseverance in not giving in to them will be worth it in the end.

Maintaining Lifestyle Changes

One of the most effective ways to prevent or overcome a dopamine relapse is to establish new, healthier habits during the process of recovery. Creating a completely different lifestyle is a good stepping stone for overcoming dopamine addiction, but it's only the beginning. To make the fasting phase successful, we must also maintain these new positive lifestyle changes. Finding triggers in unexpected places makes it harder to stay motivated to engage in activities we were initially excited about. Here are some of the factors to be aware of when trying to maintain a healthier lifestyle.

Diet

Opting for not-so-healthy dietary choices is a common side effect of addictive behavior. Unfortunately, the consequences of this dietary neglect remain long after the triggers have been removed. As you have learned in the chapter talking about dopamine diets and fats, an addict in recovery has a lot of nutrition-related challenges to overcome. However, as with many other diets, a diet of a recovering addict also comes down to implementing healthier choices and eliminating unhealthy ones.

Making proper nutritional choices improves our mood, boosts our energy levels in general, and allows our body to heal the damage caused by the addiction. All this will lower the risk of relapse, as the mind won't feel the need to reach for dopamine even when it's trying to cope with stress or depression.

Exercise

Exercise has a longer number of benefits for our health - and even more so when it comes to overcoming a dopamine addiction. Regular physical activity curbs cravings, reduce stress levels, improves self-confidence, boosts energy levels, and triggers the release of endorphins - the hormones that make us feel good without side effects. And no, this doesn't mean you have to hit the gym every day during a dopamine fasting phase. Enjoyable activities will work every time, regardless of their intensity or frequency.

For those having a hard time finding the motivation to start working out, it's a good idea to find group activities or ask some friends to join in on the sessions. This will be particularly helpful if you have never exercised before or haven't done it for a long time. In this, it's also recommended that you check in with a medical professional to assess how much exercise your body can take.

Another thing to keep in mind is that workouts can also be addictive. Compulsive patterns of exercise can not only cause an injury, but they might trigger a dopamine relapse and set back the recovery for a considerable time.

Mental Health

Taking care of your mental health is one of the most challenging parts of the journey, but it's also the most important one. Unpleasant emotions often trigger dopamine relapse. Anxiety, fear, anger, depression, sadness, and even boredom can lead to a need for something more. Monitoring our mood allows us to catch these feelings as soon as they arise and counteract them.

There are several ways to deal with a negative emotional state, including visiting a specialist addiction mental health professionals, support groups, and spending more time with supportive friends and family members. Sometimes, the recovery requires the person to be assessed and treated for medical conditions, whether these were caused by the addiction or not. Engaging in activities we enjoy is another great way to keep our mental health in check.

Dealing with Stress

Stress is a huge contributor to mental health issues and a possible dopamine relapse. Taking a proactive approach to managing stressful situations will make it easier to recover from an addiction. The first step in this is learning to recognize the symptoms of stress. Depending on their origin, the symptoms can include racing thoughts, troubles with focusing, irritability, headaches, chest pain, muscle tension, alternated sleeping and eating patterns.

Having identified the most common stressors in our lives, we can adopt some techniques to prevent and deal with this emotional state. Here, the key is to find something we enjoy and fit in our new, healthier lifestyle.

Sleep Habits

Getting enough quality sleep can help the mind feel rested, which, in turn, will make it less vulnerable to a relapse. The better the mind functions, the less likely the body will experience withdrawal symptoms. Going to bed around the same time every night and not using any mind-stimulating product will allow it to stay relaxed during the entire night. Making it a priority to create an environment where we aren't disturbed during our sleep is also essential for coping with relapse.

Changing Your Environment

Our environment plays a huge role in our recovery. The people in our lives, the dynamics, and physical surroundings themselves can determine the likelihood of dopamine relapse during or after the fasting phase. Here are some of the ways our environment impacts our recovery journey:

- Unresolved issues from childhood can trigger addictive behavior

- Unhealthy family dynamics often intensify stressful situations

- Current social environments may facilitate relapse

- Stressful work environment can also trigger the need for dopamine

- Digital technology can be very distracting during recovery

- Physical environment also contribute to poor mental health

The obvious solution to changing these factors in our environment isn't always easy. We can't always afford to change our workplace just because there are too many triggers involved in it. Nor can we cut off connections with all our family members that remind us of childhood trauma. But some factors we have influence over, and the current social circle is one of them.

Changing Social Environment

It can be tempting to go back to the pleasure-seeking behavior if those around us are also engaged in similar conduct. Whether it's an addictive substance or digital technology, if everyone else around you is using it, this can cause you to fall back into the old loop once more. On the other hand, avoiding the old circle often comes with guilt, which may cause the triggers to emerge. Spending too much time alone also leaves us with ample time to contemplate using the source of addiction again. So, the most obvious solution is to build a new social network with people who don't engage in this behavior. Spending time around people who, instead of draining your energy, are supporting you will allow you to make positive changes.

Committing to Goals

Committing to long-term goals is a great way to stay focused on other things than the source of our addiction. It takes careful planning of regular schedules for the days, weeks, and months it will take us to achieve our goal. This will also make it easier to avoid triggers in your routine.

Find the most ambitious (but still feasible) goal you can think of, and start working towards it. Break it down to smaller milestones and create a timetable for revising them. It's also a good idea to take the individual tasks in these milestones and incorporate them into the schedule, wherever you have free time. For example, if you know that you would usually engage in addictive behavior after lunchtime or work, give yourself an important task for this period.

This will leave you with less time to have a relapse, but having more things to do may feel overwhelming at first. However, as you reach your individual milestones and get closer to your end goal, you will feel more satisfied with your decisions.

Finding Motivation

If you have just started dopamine fasting, you may still feel like your life is in shambles. While this is entirely normal, it does little to inspire you to continue your recovery journey. Even if you have been fasting for a while, the constant challenges can leave you less than satisfied with yourself. Feeling like you are wasting a lot of time can be incredibly unmotivating - and only a powerful desire to change will help overcome this.

It's not a question of whether you need to leave an addiction behind, but whether you want to. As mentioned before, dopamine fasting can be pretty uncomfortable, so motivation is key to success. But in the end, you must remember that it will be worth it, and with a proper approach, you can make the process easier than you think. Going back to the previous addictive behavior is never an option. However, if you find the habits too hard to maintain, you can always modify them to fit your needs even more. The key is to do this without triggering a dopamine release.

Avoiding Boredom

For people recovering from an addiction, boredom is one of the most dangerous feelings to have. Being bored causes us to isolate ourselves, engage in hazardous (and addictive) behavior and spend time and money we can't afford. Therefore, it stands to reason that avoiding boredom is elemental for success in recovery. Fortunately, there are countless ways to chase away boredom without endangering our mental or physical health. Trying out new, productive, or fun activities is always helpful. Or, if you aren't sure which activities may be suitable for your recovery process, you can always reach out to support groups for some suggestions.

Key Takeaways

- Learning to recognize and manage triggering situations plays an essential role in our recovery journey. It teaches us that addictive behavior is no longer the solution to uncomfortable feelings, situations, and thoughts.

- To increase our chances for success and make the changes we need, we often need to start with our environment - as this is where most triggers lie.

- Once our environment is trigger-free, adopting and maintaining healthier lifestyle changes will further promote our recovery.

- Maintaining a healthy lifestyle is another huge part of successfully overcoming a dopamine relapse.

- Committing to our most ambitious, long-term goals keeps us focused on productive endeavors and reduces our chances of engaging in unproductive and addictive behavior.

- We must be ready for surprises, particularly the negative ones capable of evoking stress and triggering a relapse even with careful planning.

- We must prepare for a long journey because a short dopamine fasting phase rarely does the trick.

- It's normal to lose motivation from time to time, but we can always find it again in different activities. The key is to avoid boredom as much as possible.

8

Dopamine and ADHD

ADHD (attention deficit hyperactivity disorder) has been linked to dopamine in many ways. The level of dopamine may be lower than normal in people with ADHD, making it harder for them to control certain behaviors and stay focused. And because the stimulant medication works by increasing dopamine levels, this supports the idea that lower dopamine levels could cause ADHD symptoms.

It's almost like having a hole in your dopamine bucket when you have ADHD and can't seem to get things done. The more you try to fill the bucket up with rewards, the more you will find yourself searching for more and more rewards. This is where your distractions and hobbies come in. They can help to fill that dopamine bucket up in a healthy way and help you to focus on what's important.

It can be tough to manage, but you can do it like a pro with a little bit of knowledge and some helpful strategies. This chapter will teach you how to find and use your distractions and hobbies to help manage your ADHD. It provides an in-depth look at how dopamine can be affected by ADHD. You will also learn about different types of distractions and hobbies and how to find the ones that work best for you. Managing ADHD can seem like a daunting task, but it doesn't have to be with the help of this chapter.

Our Non-ADHD Brain

We have a dopamine system that helps us focus on tasks. It helps us ignore distractions and stay motivated and engaged in our work. This same system helps us feel pleasure from our hobbies and interests and can be triggered by something good happening to us, for example, doing our work like getting a promotion or praise from others or simply completing our work. But it can also be triggered by completely unrelated activities, such as eating something sweet, watching a funny video online, or winning at a game.

The ADHD Brain

Our brains are wired differently if we have ADHD. Our brain's ability to focus on the activity at hand is impaired; it cannot easily ignore other stimuli or competing interests even if they are less important than what we are trying to accomplish. Our dopamine system is also more easily triggered by other things besides completing tasks or achieving goals related to our work. This means that we may be more likely to seek out distractions and other pleasures that stimulate our dopamine systems rather than stay focused on the task at hand until it is complete.

Dopamine plays an important role in how we feel pleasure, but it's also involved in learning, memory, and motor system function. The ADHD condition makes it hard for you to focus and follow directions. You may forget things quickly or act impulsively. In children with ADHD, symptoms occur at a young age and are usually present for over six months or longer. Children with ADHD have trouble staying focused and paying attention. They may be hyperactive (overactive) or have difficulty controlling impulsive behaviors (can't wait their turn).

As we have learned, dopamine is the "feel-good hormone" released as part of the reward system when you do something enjoyable, such as eating delicious food or achieving a goal. Dopamine helps regulate and control movement and emotions. It also aids cognitive functions like focusing and memory. When dopamine is released, it causes several physiological changes in the body, including increased heart rate and blood pressure.

How Is Dopamine Affected by ADHD?

A neurotransmitter responsible for transmitting signals between the brain's nerve cells is involved in many different functions, including movement, pleasure, attention, and learning.

ADHD has been linked to dopamine in many ways. For one, ADHD can impair the brain's ability to focus and ignore distractions. This makes it difficult to stay on task and can lead to a lack of productivity. ADHD can also make it difficult to control impulsive behaviors, leading to problems with relationships, school, and work.

On a more positive note, people with ADHD may be more creative and innovative due to their increased ability to develop new ideas. They may also be more emotionally sensitive and more likely to empathize with others.

Studies have also shown that people with ADHD have a harder time getting pleasure from activities that usually produce a dopamine rush. This may be because the dopamine receptors in their brains are not as sensitive as those of people without ADHD. This could explain why people with ADHD are more likely to seek out distractions and hobbies that produce a dopamine rush. Here are a few of the most common dopamine-related problems seen in people with ADHD:

1. **Difficulty Focusing and Staying on Task**

   One of the most common symptoms of ADHD is difficulty focusing and staying on task. When someone with ADHD is trying to focus, their brain is not getting the dopamine it needs to keep them focused long enough on a task to get the pleasure signal. So, they end up leaving the work or activity and jumping to the next one, which could be anything that has distracted them. And this cycle repeats itself until the condition can be managed.

2. Impulsive Behavior

People with ADHD may act impulsively because of low levels of dopamine. This impulsiveness can cause problems in relationships, at work, and other life areas. Dopamine is involved in the brain's "stop" or "slow down" system, and low dopamine levels can lead to a lack of inhibition and an inability to control impulsive behavior.

3. Difficulty Handling Stress

People with ADHD often find it harder to handle stress, resulting in displays of anxiety, anger, and depression. When people with ADHD feel stressed, their dopamine levels drop even further, making it harder to cope. This can lead to a vicious cycle where stress causes dopamine levels to drop, and low dopamine levels cause more stress.

4. Sensitivity to Rewards

People with ADHD may be more sensitive to rewards than people without ADHD. They find it easier to get motivated and stay focused when they know there is a reward at the end of the task. This could be because dopamine is involved in the brain's reward system. When people with ADHD get a rush of dopamine from a reward, they are more likely to be motivated to do the task again.

5. **Craving Novelty**

People with ADHD may be more likely to seek new and exciting experiences than those without ADHD. This could be because they need more dopamine to feel satisfied. The brain's pleasure center, or nucleus acumens, is activated by activities that produce a dopamine rush. This explains why people with ADHD are more likely to crave new experiences and find it harder to stick to the same routine.

Chasing Dopamine

We all have our distractions and hobbies. One of the great benefits of ADHD is that we're good at finding things to do. But how many of these activities are making you happy? How many are only making you feel momentarily content? The answer to these questions could be the difference between life-changing happiness and frustrating mediocrity.

The brain chemical dopamine plays a part in motivation and the pleasure principle. It's believed to be partly responsible for cravings, addictions, and "reward-seeking behavior." The more dopamine there is in your brain, the better you feel — but it doesn't last long. Interestingly, too much dopamine can cause depression or apathy if it's released too quickly or too often. This is why some ADHD medications have been shown to improve mood by slowing the production of excess amounts of dopamine.

If you have ADHD, you may be familiar with "hyperfocus" — when your mind gets stuck on something that interests you, to the point where it's difficult to focus on other tasks. A study done by researchers at Stanford University found that people with ADHD release much more dopamine than normal people when they hyper-focus on a task they enjoy doing. It's thought that this excessive dopamine release may be why people with ADHD find it so hard to focus on other tasks.

So, how can you use this information to your advantage?

1. **Understand Your Triggers**

   Know what makes you feel good and what makes you feel bad. When you know what triggers your dopamine rush, you can avoid the things that make you feel bad and focus on the things that make you feel good. Avoid stress whenever possible and find ways to relax. Give yourself time to do the things you enjoy without feeling guilty.

2. **Set Goals and Rewards**

   When you have a goal, it's easier to focus on the task at hand. Give yourself a dopamine rush by setting achievable goals and rewarding yourself for reaching them. Make sure your rewards are something you enjoy, like spending time with friends, going for a walk, or watching your favorite movie. However, be aware that too many rewards can have the opposite effect and lower your dopamine levels. Find a balance between too many and too few rewards.

3. **Take Breaks**

When you feel yourself getting stressed, take a break. Relax your mind and body with some deep breathing or a short walk. Meditate, if that's your thing. Just make sure you're not over-scheduling yourself and leaving no time for breaks. A healthy mind means a healthy dopamine level. The recommended break time is 5-10 minutes for every 20-30 minutes of work. Set a timer if you need to.

4. Stay Balanced

Dopamine is a motivator, but it can also be addictive. Don't overdo it on the things that make you feel good, or you'll end up feeling bad. Don't become so obsessed with a single activity that you neglect other important areas of your life. Find a balance between work and play, between alone time and socializing, and between excitement and stability.

5. Seek Out New Experiences

Dopamine is released in response to new experiences. If you want to feel good, explore new things. Try something you've never done before. Take a different route to work, eat something new for dinner, travel to a new place. The more new experiences you have, the more dopamine your brain will produce. Doing something different every day can keep your dopamine levels high and your life exciting. And, who knows, you might even find some new interests in the process.

6. Avoid Stimulants

While some people with ADHD find relief from stimulant medications, others find them to be addictive and damaging to their dopamine levels. If you're struggling with addiction, find a support group or therapist who can help you get your life back on track. Don't try to fix things on your own. Get help from professionals when you're struggling with dopamine-related problems.

7. Exercise

Exercise is one of the best ways to boost your dopamine levels. It not only releases dopamine, but it also releases endorphins, which make you feel good. Exercise also helps to improve focus and concentration. If you can't find the time to work out, try going for a walk or taking a bike ride. Anything that gets your body moving is good for your dopamine levels.

8. Eat Healthy Foods

What you put into your body directly impacts your dopamine levels. Eat foods high in protein and healthy fats, like nuts and seeds. Avoid processed foods and sugary snacks. Eat plenty of fruits and vegetables, especially leafy greens. Drink plenty of water and avoid caffeine and alcohol. When you eat healthy foods, you're giving your body the nutrients it needs to produce dopamine.

9. Get Enough Sleep

Your brain needs time to rest and rejuvenate. If you're not getting enough sleep, your dopamine levels will drop. The recommended amount of sleep is 7-8 hours per night. If you're having trouble sleeping, make sure your bedroom is dark, quiet, and cool. Avoid watching television or working on the computer in bed. Reserve your bed for sleep only.

10. Practice Mindfulness

Mindfulness is the practice of being aware of your thoughts and feelings in the present moment. When you're mindful, you're not judging or criticizing yourself. You're just observing what's going on without attaching any judgments or emotions to it. Mindfulness can help you to become more aware of your dopamine levels. When you're aware of what's happening at the moment, you can make better choices about how to manage your dopamine.

11. Stay Positive

When you're positive, you're more likely to take action and achieve your goals. Stay positive even when things are tough. While positivity breeds dopamine, negativity breeds stress and anxiety, damaging your dopamine levels. Don't let negative thoughts take over your life. Stay positive and focused on your goals.

12. Use Technology to Your Advantage

Technology can be a helpful tool for managing dopamine levels. Many apps and websites can help you to track your moods and emotions. Technology can also help you connect with others struggling with dopamine-related issues. There are many support groups and forums available online that can help you to find information and support. Use technology to your advantage and find resources that will help you to manage your dopamine levels.

13. Let Go of Perfectionism

Perfectionism can be damaging to your dopamine levels. When you're a perfectionist, you're always putting pressure on yourself to achieve often unrealistic goals. This can lead to stress and anxiety, lowering your dopamine levels. If you're struggling with perfectionism, try to let it go, accept yourself for who you are, and focus on your strengths. Don't compare yourself to others. When you let go of perfectionism, you'll relax and enjoy life more.

14. Counteract Negative Emotions

Try to counteract those feelings with positive emotions when you're feeling down, anxious, or stressed. Exercise, eat healthy foods and get enough sleep. Spend time with positive people who make you feel good. Listen to upbeat music or watch funny movies. Do things that make you happy and that raise your dopamine levels. You'll have more energy and be more productive when you feel good.

15. Adopt a Support Animal

A support animal can be a great way to manage dopamine levels. Pets can help reduce stress and anxiety, helping you maintain your dopamine levels. They can also provide companionship and love, which can help to boost your dopamine levels. If you're considering getting a support animal, do some research to find an animal that would be a good fit for you. Many different types of animals can serve as support animals, so find one that would make you happy.

16.Go On Treks

Hiking, camping, and other outdoor activities can be ideal ways to raise your dopamine levels. You're surrounded by nature when you're outdoors, which can be calming and peaceful. You're also getting exercise, which is good for your body and mind. Spending time in nature is also a boost to your dopamine levels, and it improves your mood.

17. Join a Support Group

If you're struggling with dopamine-related issues, joining a support group can be a great way to get help. Many groups are available online and in-person that cater to people with dopamine-related issues. Support groups can provide you with information, support, and solidarity. They can also help you connect with others who are going through the same thing. If you're struggling, consider joining a support group.

18.Get a Massage

Massages can be a great way to raise your dopamine levels. Massages can help to reduce stress and anxiety, which can lower your dopamine levels. They can also help to improve your mood and increase your energy levels. If you're feeling stressed out, consider getting a massage. It can be a great way to relax and boost your dopamine levels.

19. Take a Vacation

When you're feeling stressed or overwhelmed, take a vacation if you can. A change of scenery can do wonders to help manage dopamine levels. Going on a vacation helps to refresh you and give you a new perspective. It can also help you to relax and enjoy life more. If you're feeling stressed, consider taking a vacation. It can be a great way to boost your dopamine levels.

20.   Find a Focus Method That Works for You

Many different focus methods can work for people with ADHD. Some people prefer to work in short bursts, while others prefer to work for longer periods. Some people like to work with noise distractions, while others prefer to work in silence. Find a focus method that works for you and stick with it.

21. Create a Routine

When you have ADHD, it's important to create a routine. Having a routine will help you to stay organized and focused. It will also help you to stay on track with your goals. You know what to expect each day when you have a routine, and you can plan.

22.   Seek Professional Help

If you're struggling to manage your dopamine levels, consider seeking professional help. Many professionals specialize in this area. They can help you to understand what's going on and give you tools to manage your condition.

Dopamine is essential for focus, motivation, and productivity. When your dopamine levels are balanced, you'll be able to focus and accomplish tasks. These tips will help you manage your ADHD like a pro.

Key Takeaways

This chapter was all about dopamine and how it affects people with ADHD. Here are the key takeaways:

- Impulsive behaviors, lack of focus, and problems with motivation are all symptoms of ADHD caused by low dopamine levels.

- Understanding triggers and managing dopamine levels can help people with ADHD to live more productive lives.

- Seeking new hobbies and distractions can help to raise dopamine levels.

- There are many different ways to manage dopamine levels, including getting regular exercise, spending time in nature, joining a support group, getting a massage, and taking a vacation.

- Getting a massage, going on a vacation, and joining a support group can also help to raise dopamine levels.

- Creating a routine can help people with ADHD stay on track and organized since you know what to expect each day and plan.

- If you're struggling to manage your dopamine levels, consider seeking professional help. Many professionals specialize in dopamine-related issues.

This guide has outlined everything you need to know about dopamine and ADHD. Managing dopamine levels is essential for people with ADHD, and the tips in this guide will help you to do just that. With a little bit of effort, you can manage your ADHD like a pro.

Every person is different, and what works for one person may not work for another. Be sure to experiment with different methods and find what works best for you. The tips in this guide are a great starting point but don't be afraid to get creative and find what works best for you.

Afterword

Dopamine is a very important neurotransmitter responsible for many functions in the brain. When dopamine levels get too high or too low, it can lead to addiction, ADHD, and other mental health conditions. A dopamine detox is a way to help restore balance to the dopamine levels in the brain. This can be done through different techniques such as dopamine fasting, diets, and supplementary exercises. There are also many ways to overcome a relapse if it occurs. A dopamine detox can be a very beneficial method to improve overall mental health and well-being and start you on the road to recovery from addiction.

This book covered everything you need to know about dopamine and dopamine detox. The first chapter talked about dopamine's role in the brain and how it can become imbalanced. We saw the chemical role of dopamine from an evolutionary standpoint and how dopamine gets abused with technology in the modern age. The second chapter discussed the science of addiction and how dopamine is involved. It covered environmental and biological factors that increase addiction.

The third chapter talked about the most common dopamine addictions and provided tips on how to overcome them. It explained how they manifest and their detox, including withdrawal and timeframes. The fourth chapter discussed dopamine fasting, diets, and their benefits. It discussed how to adjust nutrition for dopamine fasting and covered the various diets to help detox dopamine.

The fifth chapter covered the benefits of a successful dopamine detox. These include increased productivity, healthier relationships, overall happier and uplifted mood. The sixth chapter talked about techniques and strategies for detoxing the brain's dopamine production with the help of daily meditation, cold showers, mindful eating, getting exercise, socializing, being with friends and family, and digesting long-form content.

The seventh chapter discussed relapse prevention, including identifying dopamine cravings, dealing with triggers, and getting back on track after a relapse. It discussed how to improve your life and achieve your most ambitious objectives by learning how to establish healthy long-term habits, cope with unexpected setbacks, and remain motivated.

The last chapter talked about dopamine and ADHD. It explained how dopamine affects ADHD symptoms and how to manage them. It showed how ADHD is caused by a dopamine imbalance and how it can be treated with detox. Remember, if you are considering a dopamine detox, speak with a healthcare professional first. They can help you decide if this is the right choice for you and can provide guidance on how to best go about it.

So, there you have it – a dopamine detox! It can be a little daunting to think about, even harder to do successfully, but it's worth it in the long run. And you come to realize that you are not alone with these issues. You can overcome addiction, ADHD, and other imbalance-related issues by detoxing your dopamine. If you are considering a dopamine detox, this book is a great place to start. It provides all the information you need to get started and to make the most out of your detox. Follow the steps in this guide, and you'll soon be on your way to a healthy, balanced dopamine system. Good luck!

References

Cookie consent and choices. (n.d.). Retrieved from
https://www.npr.org/sections/health-shots/2021/08/25/1030930259/in-
dopamine-nation-overabundance-keeps-u-s-craving-more

Dopamine functions. (2010, January 10). News-Medical.Net.
https://www.news-medical.net/health/Dopamine-Functions.aspx

Dopamine, Smartphones & You: A battle for your time. (2018, May 1).
Science in the News. https://sitn.hms.harvard.edu/flash/2018/dopamine-
smartphones-battle-time/

Dresp-Langley, B. (2020). Children's health in the digital age. International
Journal of Environmental Research and Public Health, 17(9).
https://doi.org/10.3390/ijerph17093240

Effects of dopamine: How dopamine drives human behavior. (2019,
September 5). Into Action Recovery Centers.
https://www.intoactionrecovery.com/how-dopamine-drives-our-behavior/

Gibbons, A. (2018). Dopamine may have given humans our social edge over
other apes. Science (New York, N.Y.).
https://doi.org/10.1126/science.aat0850

Konkel, L., & Jasmer, R. (n.d.). Dopamine: A neurotransmitter.
EverydayHealth.Com. Retrieved from
https://www.everydayhealth.com/dopamine/

McNamara, B. (2021, November 10). The science behind social media's hold
on our mental health. Teen Vogue. https://www.teenvogue.com/story/the-
science-behind-social-medias-hold-on-our-mental-health

Parkin, S. (2018, March 4). Has dopamine got us hooked on tech? The
Guardian. https://www.theguardian.com/technology/2018/mar/04/has-
dopamine-got-us-hooked-on-tech-facebook-apps-addiction

Pietrangelo, A. (2019, November 5). Dopamine effects on the body, plus drug and hormone interactions. Healthline. https://www.healthline.com/health/dopamine-effects

Technology addiction and the brain: Understanding the impact. (2021, March 22). StoneRidge: Center for Brains. https://pronghornpsych.com/technology-addiction-and-the-brain/

Waters, J. (2021, August 22). Constant craving: how digital media turned us all into dopamine addicts. The Guardian. https://www.theguardian.com/global/2021/aug/22/how-digital-media-turned-us-all-into-dopamine-addicts-and-what-we-can-do-to-break-the-cycle

What is dopamine? (n.d.). WebMD. Retrieved from https://www.webmd.com/mental-health/what-is-dopamine

Yamaguchi, Y., Lee, Y.-A., & Goto, Y. (2015). Dopamine in socioecological and evolutionary perspectives: implications for psychiatric disorders. Frontiers in Neuroscience, 9, 219. https://doi.org/10.3389/fnins.2015.00219

Yamamoto, K., & Vernier, P. (2011). The evolution of dopamine systems in chordates. Frontiers in Neuroanatomy, 5, 21. https://doi.org/10.3389/fnana.2011.00021

(N.d.). Apa.Org. Retrieved from https://www.apa.org/news/podcasts/speaking-of-psychology/dopamine

22 reasons people use drugs and alcohol. (2021, March 31). 12 Keys. https://www.12keysrehab.com/22-reasons-people-use-drugs-and-alcohol/

Ariane Resnick, C. N. C. (n.d.). Can you be addicted to dopamine? Verywell Mind. Retrieved from https://www.verywellmind.com/can-you-get-addicted-to-dopamine-5207433

Asensio, S., Hernández-Rabaza, V., & Orón Semper, J. V. (2020). What is the "trigger" of addiction? Frontiers in Behavioral Neuroscience, 14, 54. https://doi.org/10.3389/fnbeh.2020.00054

Drugs and mental health. (2015, August 7). Mental Health Foundation. https://www.mentalhealth.org.uk/a-to-z/d/drugs-and-mental-health

Felman, A. (2021, April 23). Addiction: Definition, symptoms, withdrawal, and treatment. Medicalnewstoday.Com. https://www.medicalnewstoday.com/articles/323465

Hartney, E., BSc, MSc, & MA. (n.d.). 5 triggers of relapse and how to avoid them. Verywell Mind. Retrieved from https://www.verywellmind.com/why-did-i-relapse-21900

Healthdirect Australia. (2021). What is addiction? https://www.healthdirect.gov.au/what-is-addiction

Huett, K. (2020, August 24). The science behind addiction. National Association of Addiction Treatment Providers. https://www.naatp.org/addiction-treatment-resources/understanding-addiction

National Institute on Drug Abuse. (n.d.-a). Drug misuse and addiction. National Institute on Drug Abuse. Retrieved from https://nida.nih.gov/publications/drugs-brains-behavior-science-addiction/drug-misuse-addiction

National Institute on Drug Abuse. (n.d.-b). Preface. National Institute on Drug Abuse. Retrieved from https://nida.nih.gov/publications/drugs-brains-behavior-science-addiction/preface

National Institute on Drug Abuse. (2018, June 6). Understanding drug use and addiction DrugFacts. National Institute on Drug Abuse. https://nida.nih.gov/publications/drugfacts/understanding-drug-use-addiction

National Institute on Drug Abuse. (2020, May 26). The science of drug use: A resource for the justice sector. National Institute on Drug Abuse. https://nida.nih.gov/drug-topics/criminal-justice/science-drug-use-resource-justice-sector

NHS website. (n.d.). Addiction: what is it? Nhs.Uk. Retrieved from https://www.nhs.uk/live-well/healthy-body/addiction-what-is-it/

Raypole, C. (2019, April 30). Dopamine addiction: A guide to dopamine's role in addiction. Healthline. https://www.healthline.com/health/dopamine-addiction

The science behind addiction. (n.d.). Americanaddictioncenters.Org. Retrieved from https://americanaddictioncenters.org/learn/science-behind-addiction/

The science of addiction. (n.d.). Shatterproof.Org. Retrieved from https://www.shatterproof.org/learn/addiction-basics/science-of-addiction

The science of addiction. (2019, August 9). SAFE Project. https://www.safeproject.us/resource/science-of-addiction/

The science of drug use and addiction: The basics. (n.d.). Drugabuse.Gov. Retrieved from https://archives.drugabuse.gov/publications/media-guide/science-drug-use-addiction-basics

The top 7 reasons why people start doing drugs. (n.d.). Newlife360inc.Com. Retrieved from https://newlife360inc.com/blog/why-do-people-do-drugs

Understanding triggers and how to deal with them in recovery. (2019, December 29). Agape Treatment Center. https://www.agapetc.com/understanding-triggers-and-how-to-deal-with-them-in-recovery/

Why do people use alcohol and other drugs? (n.d.). Org.Au. Retrieved from https://adf.org.au/insights/why-do-people-use-alcohol-and-other-drugs/

Why do people use drugs? How do drugs work? - drug-free world. (2010, July 9).

Wise, R. A., & Robble, M. A. (2020). Dopamine and addiction. Annual Review of Psychology, 71(1), 79–106. https://doi.org/10.1146/annurev-psych-010418-103337

(N.d.-a). Indiatimes.Com. Retrieved from https://timesofindia.indiatimes.com/life-style/health-fitness/health-news/the-psychology-behind-drug-misuse-why-do-people-take-drugs-long-term-health-risks-and-all-you-need-to-know/photostory/86802379.cms

(N.d.-b). Apa.Org. Retrieved from https://dictionary.apa.org/trigger

Adinoff, B. (2004). Neurobiologic processes in drug reward and addiction. Harvard Review of Psychiatry, 12(6), 305–320. https://doi.org/10.1080/10673220490910844

Brookshire, B. (2013, July 3). What is dopamine for, anyway? Love, lust, pleasure, addiction? Slate. https://slate.com/technology/2013/07/what-is-dopamine-love-lust-sex-addiction-gambling-motivation-reward.html

Dopamine, Smartphones & You: A battle for your time. (2018, May 1). Science in the News. https://sitn.hms.harvard.edu/flash/2018/dopamine-smartphones-battle-time/

Powledge, T. M. (1999). Addiction and the brain. Bioscience, 49(7), 513–519. https://doi.org/10.2307/1313471

Raypole, C. (2019, April 30). Dopamine addiction: A guide to dopamine's role in addiction. Healthline. https://www.healthline.com/health/dopamine-addiction

Understanding addiction - HelpGuide.Org. (n.d.). Retrieved from https://www.helpguide.org/harvard/how-addiction-hijacks-the-brain.htm

Volkow, N. D., Fowler, J. S., Wang, G.-J., & Swanson, J. M. (2004). Dopamine in drug abuse and addiction: results from imaging studies and treatment implications. Molecular Psychiatry, 9(6), 557–569. https://doi.org/10.1038/sj.mp.4001507

Volkow, Nora D., Fowler, J. S., Wang, G.-J., Swanson, J. M., & Telang, F. (2007). Dopamine in drug abuse and addiction: results of imaging studies and treatment implications: Results of imaging studies and treatment implications. Archives of Neurology, 64(11), 1575–1579. https://doi.org/10.1001/archneur.64.11.1575

What is dopamine? (n.d.). WebMD. Retrieved from https://www.webmd.com/mental-health/what-is-dopamine

Akers, W. (2019, November 20). Is dopamine fasting a way to fix your brain or a Silicon Valley fad? Healthline Media. https://www.healthline.com/health-news/what-is-dopamine-fasting

Gillespie, C. (2019, November 14). "dopamine fasting" is supposed to help you think clearer and have more focus. Here's what to know. Health.Com. https://www.health.com/mind-body/dopamine-fasting

Grant, K. (2020, January 3). Dopamine fast: "The hunger and boredom were intense." BBC News. https://www.bbc.com/news/newsbeat-50834914

Heard about Dopamine fasting? It could be the way to make your brain work hard! (2020, August 6). Times Of India. https://timesofindia.indiatimes.com/life-style/health-fitness/de-stress/heard-about-dopamine-fasting-it-could-be-the-way-to-make-your-brain-work-hard/articleshow/77392150.cms

John M. Grohol, P. D. (2019, November 13). Dopamine fasting probably doesn't work, try this instead. Psych Central. https://psychcentral.com/blog/dopamine-fasting-probably-doesnt-work-try-this-instead

Kelleher, E. (2021, January 18). Dopamine fasting can make you a happier, more focused man. Fatherly. https://www.fatherly.com/health-science/dopamine-fasting-can-make-you-a-happier-more-focused-man/

Todd, L. (2021, June 30). Dopamine detox: How does it work? Medicalnewstoday.Com. https://www.medicalnewstoday.com/articles/dopamine-detox

Trevor Sutton, A. (2020). Silicon Valley's latest fad is dopamine fasting – and that may not be as crazy as it sounds. The Conversation. https://theconversation.com/silicon-valleys-latest-fad-is-dopamine-fasting-and-that-may-not-be-as-crazy-as-it-sounds-128849

SuccessYeti. (2021, July 27). What Is Dopamine Detox: Its Benefits. SuccessYeti. https://www.successyeti.com/health-and-fitness/what-is-dopamine-detox-its-benefits/2021/07/28

CPSIA information can be obtained
at www.ICGtesting.com
Printed in the USA
BVHW092321160922
647223BV00023B/2105